RED
ROCKS

RED
ROCKS
RACHAEL KING

RANDOM HOUSE
NEW ZEALAND

 The assistance of Creative New Zealand is gratefully acknowledged by the author and publisher.

A RANDOM HOUSE BOOK published by Random House New Zealand
18 Poland Road, Glenfield, Auckland, New Zealand

For more information about our titles go to
www.randomhouse.co.nz

A catalogue record for this book is available from the National Library of New Zealand

Random House New Zealand is part of the Random House Group
New York   London   Sydney   Auckland   Delhi   Johannesburg

First published 2012, reprinted 2013

© 2012 Rachael King

The moral rights of the author have been asserted

ISBN 978 1 86979 914 4

Cover design: Area Design
Text design: Megan van Staden
Printed and bound in Australia by Griffin Press

This publication is printed on paper pulp sourced from sustainably grown and managed forests, using Elemental Chlorine Free (EFC) bleaching, and printed with 100% vegetable-based inks.

This title is also available as an ebook

For my boys,
Thomas and Alexander.

I

Waves battered the beach, chattering to the stones as they receded. Jake stood still, watching the rocks, waiting for a movement. And there it was: a seal, with sleek, damp fur, launching itself into the water like a torpedo. He looked for it amongst the floating islands of kelp, thought he spotted it at first but no, there it was, further away. Its head surfaced and it rolled onto its back, raised one flipper as if in a wave and was gone. He wanted to climb up onto the rocks and find more, but he was scared of their angry growls and their sharp teeth. Even though they lay around like blobs all day, he knew they could move surprisingly fast, even on land.

He continued his walk towards Red Rocks. Great grey cliffs loomed beside him and the light wind bounced off them and back into his face. He pulled his jacket tighter. He didn't mind being alone. He liked walking by himself. It gave him time to think about things, but also to imagine things. When he was younger, he would have made up games, like being pursued by pirates angry at him for stealing their treasure. But he was older now, and games were for little kids. Instead he thought about his mother, back in Auckland with his half-brother Davey and her husband Greg. He liked Greg, but he also liked coming to Wellington to spend time with his dad in Owhiro Bay. His dad sometimes took him out from Island Bay in a little boat with an outboard motor — they puttered past the bright fishing boats and out around the island, the wind lashing their faces and turning their hands to ice.

What would Mum be doing now? Probably feeding the baby. Davey couldn't even crawl yet, and he would be reaching out with his grabbing hands that seemed to want to touch everything, to dig his little nails into the softest of flesh. Jake had the scratches on his cheek to prove it. The baby was pretty cute, he supposed, so he didn't mind too much. He knew better than to let Davey grab at his face, but he always looked as if he just wanted to reach out and give him a pat. Then the fist closed and the fingernails dug in and the naughty little laugh came out, guttural, like a growl.

His father was doing some work today and besides, Jake had wanted to go and explore the beach, despite the chilly, late-winter's day. He hadn't expected to come so far, but he was prepared. He sat down on a low rock and pulled out his sandwich. He imagined what his life would be like when he was a grown-up. He would be tall, like his dad, but his hair wouldn't be so dark. He'd always thought he'd be a policeman, but lately he'd been enjoying science at school, so maybe he could be a conservationist, work for Forest and Bird or Greenpeace. Something to help stop the destruction of the environment: the land and the ocean; the animals that were becoming extinct.

Jake lived in the city with his mum now, but he loved the tug of the sea air and flat horizons broken only by ships or trees. Perhaps when he grew up he would stay in one of the little shacks on this beach. He turned now to face one. It was painted grey, although it may have once been blue, faded and battered by the wind and rain. A spiral of smoke wafted up from the chimney; a pair of old black pants and a torn woollen undershirt flapped on a clothesline. Who lived here now? He wasn't wondering long. He heard a wet cough as a door on the side of the shack opened and a man stepped outside.

The man was bent and bow-legged. His white hair tufted out from under a woollen hat and he held a steaming mug in his hand as he limped over to the clothesline. With his free hand he touched the clothes, testing them to see if they were dry. Satisfied, he went to unhook the pegs but realised he needed both hands, so put the mug on the ground. He took down the undershirt first but as he moved to collect the pants his foot kicked the cup over.

'Hell and back!' the man yelled, and as he did so, his eyes found Jake sitting on his rock, watching. The flash of anger was as quickly gone and replaced by a sunny smile. The yellow-toothed grin was just as frightening as it was welcoming, but Jake knew the old man was only trying to be friendly. He waved tentatively.

'Fancy a cuppa?' yelled the man. 'I was just going to make another one for myself.'

Jake shook his head, hoping the man would go back into his house before Jake felt the need to run away.

'Suit yourself,' Jake heard him mutter as he bent with a groan to gather up the fallen mug. When he straightened he put a hand on the small of his back and grunted. And then Jake wasn't sure, but he thought he heard him say, 'The seals are better company anyway.'

Jake wasn't sure what the old man meant by this. Did he mean that he preferred the company of the seals? Or was he telling Jake to go and find the company of seals, that they were much better company than the old man?

Either way, Jake decided the old man was crazy and he was glad he hadn't accepted his offer of a cup of tea. Everyone knew that you shouldn't really talk to strangers. Especially crazy ones.

He finished his sandwich and stood up. The man had disappeared inside the house and Jake continued on his way down the beach.

At the next point, the rocks rose high and rust-red around him. They seemed to tumble off the cliffs and into the sea. Jake knew the rocks were volcanic, and he imagined lava spewing down the cliff-face and freezing as it hit the water. Even though he'd been to Red Rocks before, he always had to stop and marvel at their brightness in the grey landscape. There was something other-wordly about them; a place where magic happened.

He stopped at a rock pool to watch tiny fish flick in and out of crevices. A starfish moved lazily through the clear water. He touched tiny sea anemones and felt them kissing the tips of his fingers.

And then, as he ventured further into the rocks, something caught his eye.

At first it just looked like a solid wall, but as he got closer a fissure became apparent. It was thin at the top, barely wide enough to slip a piece of paper into, but it widened near the bottom. It was a mini cave, perfect for hiding pirate's treasure! Jake squatted down and peered inside. It was just big enough for him to crawl into if he kept his head down. He knelt on the hard ground and tiny stones dug into his knees through his jeans. Once he scrambled inside, the sound of the sea was muffled and the wind couldn't touch him. But there was a musky smell in here, strong, like the goats he had smelled on his uncle's farm. Light fell through a crack at the far end of the short tunnel, illuminating something in a corner. He reached out a hand . . . and touched fur.

Jake gave an involuntary yell and jerked his hand back, adrenaline suddenly leaping to life in his veins. He expected the growl and snap of a seal, but the tunnel remained silent. He waited. The wind outside whistled faintly against the entrance to the tunnel. Jake stretched out his hand again, tentatively this time, and when he touched soft fur, he didn't pull his hand away. There was nothing solid beneath the softness: no animal, dead or alive. Somebody had left a fur coat here, surely. He grabbed it and backed out of the tunnel, pulling the coat with him. Blinking in the light, he looked down and gasped. Without unfolding it, he knew what it was — the colour and the texture of the fur gave it away immediately. A sealskin! With disgust he realised that someone had skinned a seal. He had heard about sealers in the Antarctic, clubbing baby seals to death and stripping them on the spot, leaving their bloody, skinless carcasses staining the cold ice. The thought always made him see red — that people were capable of such cruelty. It made him ashamed to be human sometimes.

But there was no blood. He unfolded the skin and fingered the neat slit in the belly, the leathery insides. It was about his size. He could have climbed right inside it and worn it like a suit, maybe even dived into the water and twisted and tumbled in the ocean as a seal would. Instead, a powerful urge came over him. He tucked the sealskin under his arm and headed for home with his prize.

2

The sealskin was heavy. By the time Jake got home he was hot, despite the cold wind that always blew in Owhiro Bay. His dad was in his writing shed in the garden, so Jake let himself into the house and dropped the skin on his bed. Because the house was nestled in front of a steep hill, the shed was actually above the house and looked out over the bay. The road lay between the house and the sea, and sometimes when it was stormy, Jake worried that the waves would crash through the front windows of the house, but they never did.

Jake's dad wrote books about New Zealand wildlife that nobody ever read. At least, his dad joked that nobody ever read them and that was why he was so poor, living in this tiny house that was more of a shack than anything else. He rented it: he told Jake that he couldn't afford to buy waterfront property. Luckily Jake had his own room in this house — at Dad's last place, Jake had to sleep on a saggy bed in the corner of the lounge, while his dad slept and wrote in the only bedroom. He could hardly remember what it had been like when his parents were still together, but now Mum was married to Greg, who was a lawyer, things at home were more comfortable.

He didn't mind coming to stay with his father, even though Dad gave him tripe for dinner sometimes, which was just a polite word for cow's guts. And even though his dad didn't drive a flash car like Greg, he seemed happy with his life by the sea, and to Jake it was an adventure visiting him because he only had to take showers when he was really dirty, and he could go out whenever he wanted. There was no TV, which was especially boring on rainy days, but his dad always gave him good books, and he could read until midnight if he liked.

Jake knew he should probably show his dad the sealskin, but as he started towards the back door to tell him, something made him stop. He had found it, hidden, in that cave. Perhaps he shouldn't have taken it; perhaps it belonged to someone and Jake had actually stolen someone's property. His palms suddenly felt cold and sweaty, and he returned to his room and wiped them on the fur. He picked it up and hugged it to his chest. Then he got on his knees and pushed it under the bed, as far as it would go.

'Did you have a good walk?' asked his dad as he pottered around the kitchen fixing lunch. The kitchen was quite small and Dad seemed to fill every corner of it. Jake leant in the doorway, watching his dad's broad back, his thick black hair that always stood to attention.

'Yeah,' said Jake. He could say 'yeah' to his dad. His mum would have corrected him, made him say 'yes'.

'Did you see any seals?'

'Mmm . . . in the water. I saw a funny old man as well.'

His dad stopped what he was doing and turned, a knife in his hand. 'What sort of funny old man?' He looked concerned.

'Oh, not scary or anything,' said Jake. 'He was just kind of a sad old man, living in one of those cottages on the beach.'

'Really?' Dad turned around and continued cutting up tomatoes. 'I didn't think anyone lived in those. They look so abandoned. I always thought they'd be a good place to write. Or to study the seals. Hey, did I tell you?' He handed Jake a sandwich with no plate and they sat down at the dining table in the living room. 'I thought I might write about the wildlife around the south coast of Wellington for my next book. Won't have to go too far for research then!'

'Cool,' said Jake, and tucked in. They ate in silence for a while. Jake held the sandwich awkwardly as he ate, dropping tomato on the table, but his dad didn't seem to care.

'You're very quiet,' Dad said suddenly. 'Something on your mind?'

'No,' said Jake, too quickly probably. He felt himself go red. His father stared at him for a second, but must have sensed Jake's discomfort and stood up, turning back to the kitchen. 'I've got more work to do,' he said. 'We'll go to Island Bay and get fish and chips tonight, eh? What will you do for the rest of the afternoon?'

Jake shrugged. 'I might just read a book.'

After his father had gone back to the shed, Jake went back into his room to read, but he felt the sealskin calling to him. He knelt on the floor and reached under the bed. When he pulled it out, dust balls clung to it and he sneezed. It had a queer smell to it, like salt and sweat, mixed with something else he couldn't identify. It was strong, but not unpleasant. Just strange.

That evening Jake and his dad waited in the fish and chip shop for their order. They were sitting at a table looking through magazines that were years old and Jake was wondering why the owners didn't get some new ones, when something across the road caught his eye. A woman was walking up the street. She had bare feet, even though it was a cold day, and she wore an old grey coat that looked as if it had come from an op shop — it was something an old man might have worn, and it was too big for her. She had wild red hair that flashed as the late sun dodged in and out of clouds. She kept stopping, muttering to herself and turning back as if she'd forgotten something, then turning around again and travelling a few more steps. She looked too young to be crazy, much younger than his mum.

'What's she doing?' Jake asked.

Dad looked up and watched her for a few moments. 'Oh,' he said. 'That's sad. I hope she's got someone looking after her.' But as he said it, she stopped acting crazy. She drew herself taller and the windy day seemed to calm around her. She crossed the road, coming straight for the fish and chip shop! Jake looked away, buried his nose in a magazine, but suddenly she was right beside him, on the other side of the window. She cupped her hands on either side of her eyes and put her face right up to the glass. She looked around the room, without coming inside.

'She's looking for someone,' said Dad. 'I hope she finds whoever it is.' Then he smiled at the woman and Jake looked up just in time to see her give a beautiful smile back before she stepped away from the window and walked off towards the beach.

*

Jake ate too many chips, and his dreams that night were wild. He woke up sweating with a pain in his gut, but he couldn't remember what he'd been dreaming — all he knew was that the red-haired woman had been in it and so had the sealskin. The old man from the beach had been shouting something at him that he couldn't hear. He picked up the torch his dad had given him and leant over the side of the bed. The skin was still there. Its empty eyes stared mournfully at him. He got up and went through to his dad, who rumbled in his sleep, snoring. Jake shone the torch on him and the snoring stopped abruptly as his dad sat up.

'Hey, buddy.' His father's voice was full of sleep and he put a hand up to shade his eyes. 'What's up? Can you turn that off?'

Jake turned the torch off and the room fell into darkness, with only a faint orange glow from a distant street light.

'My stomach hurts,' said Jake, and as he said it, he felt like he was four years old again.

His dad leant over and opened a drawer beside his bed. He pulled out a tube and popped a tablet out.

'Here,' he said, holding it out. 'Antacid. It'll make you feel better.'

Jake put it in his mouth and chewed. It was like eating mint-flavoured chalk. He didn't want to go back to his own room. His dad seemed to know; he pulled back the covers and moved over. Jake was glad his father didn't tell him he was too old to share his bed as he stretched the blanket up to his ears and closed his eyes.

3

Jake was vaguely aware of his father getting up in the morning. The short, thin curtains blocked out none of the light, so he put the pillow over his head and went back to sleep. Dad had always got up early. Usually by the time Jake sat down for breakfast, his father would have been for a walk along the beach and then written for two hours. Dad said it was so they could spend some time together during the day without him worrying about his work, but Jake knew that he still worried about it anyway. He would sometimes stop what they were doing, holding onto the ball, or the dice, depending on the game, and his face would become vacant, as though he had left his body behind and popped off somewhere else for a few seconds.

'Your turn,' Jake would have to say. '*Dad.*' And his father would smile and keep on playing as if nothing had happened.

This morning, Jake got up to the smell of something delicious frying in the kitchen. Dad was listening to the radio, humming along to a piece of classical music.

'What time is it?' Jake peeked into the frying pan and saw pieces of dark sausage cooking next to an egg. Black pudding. Yuck. He used to like the taste of it, until he'd found out what it was made of: blood.

'It's nine o'clock, sleepyhead!' Dad rumpled his hair and pushed him towards the table. Jake sat down as his father tipped the contents of the pan onto a plate and set it in front of him. 'Careful,' he said. 'It's hot.'

'Aren't you having any?' Jake asked.

'I had porridge earlier. Besides, I know how much you like black pudding and there was only enough for one.'

Jake couldn't refuse it now. Dad was looking so pleased with himself. Gross. He forced himself to put a piece in his mouth. If he closed his eyes and pretended it was regular sausage, he could enjoy the taste without thinking about it.

'Hey, I pumped up the tyres on your old bike,' Dad said. 'You can take it out for a spin if you want.'

This cheered Jake up. There was nothing he liked more than riding along the road by the sea, especially with the wind at his back.

What Jake hadn't counted on was the southerly. He always forgot about it until it hit, which was often. There was nothing between this part of the coast and Antarctica, as his dad often reminded him, so the wind was laced with ice, and any part of him that was exposed to it quickly became numb. Sometimes Jake fancied he could smell penguins and hear the bark of husky dogs on the breeze. It wasn't strong today, but it was enough to make him take a sharp intake of breath as he rounded the first corner. He pushed on anyway, pulling the sleeves of his hoodie down over his hands, so he was riding with paws instead of fingers on the handlebars.

He had planned to bike to the Island Bay shops, maybe see if there was a movie on at the Empire, but once he was out the gate, it was as if the bike had other ideas. He felt the pull of the cliffs again, the beach with its talking stones and seals, the old man in the shack. But as he rode past the houses of Dad's neighbours, something didn't seem right. Two boys stood at the gate to a house that had always cheered Jake up when he walked past it. The cottage was painted blue and sparkling white, and the garden had a lot of windmills in it, which in the usual blustery weather would spin crazily. Some of them were in the shape of birds with funny faces, their wings whirling madly. All of them were painted to match the house. Sometimes a smiling Labrador would be in the front yard, playing. It would hide behind the lavender bushes and jump out at the windmills, barking and lolling its tongue. It never seemed to tire of the game, and Jake never tired of watching it play.

As Jake got closer to the house, he could hear the dog barking, but it wasn't a happy bark. Its yelps were high-pitched and troubled. What was going on? Whatever it was, it wasn't good. One of the boys, with dark wavy hair and an oversized brown hoodie, was holding a rope. At the other end of the rope, on the other side of the fence, the dog thrashed and howled. It was as if they had lassoed him, with the rope making a tight noose around his neck.

'Hey, Mark! Pull him closer!' The other boy, with blonde spiky hair, had a handful of stones.

'He won't bite, he's too soft.'

Jake stopped a safe distance away. Mark, the brown-haired boy, was intent on pulling the rope, but the blonde boy caught sight of him. He pulled himself up to his full height, which was much taller than Jake.

'What are you looking at, loser?'

Jake's voice was small. 'Nothing.'

A stone zinged through the air and struck him on the shoulder.

'Get outta here and mind your own business,' hissed the dark-haired boy, while his friend sniggered and pretended to hoist another missile. Jake ducked and the boys laughed. His cheeks burned and he got back on his bike and pedalled away. He didn't look at the dog as he passed, couldn't bear to see its face.

'You tell anyone and we'll get you!'

Jake ducked his head and another stone whistled past his shoulder.

What could he have done? Nothing, he told himself. The dog would be all right. Surely its owner wasn't far away. His shoulder throbbed where the stone had hit. There was nothing he could do — was there? A sick feeling crept into his stomach.

He knew boys like that, back home. Three in particular regularly stopped him on the way home from school and pushed him around a bit before getting bored and moving on to younger kids. They told him he lived in make-believe land; they called him 'retarded'; sometimes they hit him, but he always made up some excuse if the bruises showed, told his mum he'd been hit by a ball playing cricket, so she wouldn't worry. He didn't want her to march into the school, which would give the boys something else to bully him about. He thought if he just kept out of their way and didn't make trouble they would eventually forget about him. Besides, he did sometimes live in a make-believe world — they were right about that. It was much more interesting than the real world, and much safer.

He put his head down and pedalled hard, trying to push the dog, and the boys — all of them — out of his mind.

Once he left the sealed road, it was harder to pedal, but the tyres had thick tread and they took the bump and lurch of the road well. The road ran the length of the beach, all the way to Red Rocks. He put his head down against the breeze, trying not to imagine his ears freezing and breaking off. He passed a man and a woman walking the same way. The man had a backpack with a baby in it, rugged up against the cold so only its little face poked out, like a marsupial in a pouch. They had on sturdy walking shoes and polar fleece jackets, much more sensible than Jake's sneakers and hoodie.

Jake concentrated on the sound of his wheels, shush-shush-shushing on the muddy road, and the waves washing onto the stones, continuing their conversation from yesterday. He imagined the sea taunting the stones with tales of its adventures, while the stones had to make do with staying still. He imagined stories of mermaids and sailing ships, of sharp-toothed fish and whales the size of houses. He would have liked to have found a boat washed up on the shore. He would jump in it and let the sea carry him wherever it liked.

He was so engrossed in his thoughts that he didn't notice he was getting closer to the old man's shack until he was right up next to it. The old man was standing outside again, but this time he wasn't alone. A young woman stood beside him. It was the same woman from the fish and chip shop. Jake's stomach gave a little flip when he saw her; he wasn't sure why. He wondered if she had walked all that way, in bare feet. Her feet must be bruised and cut from the sharp stones.

She looked miserable. Her shoulders were hunched and she was grabbing at the old man's hands. She seemed to be pleading with him. Her bright red hair sprang in the breeze. Jake thought it might take right off into the air and carry her with it. Her oversized men's coat and pants would billow in the wind, while her bare feet would be the last he saw of her before she disappeared into the sky.

But she didn't float away. Instead, the old man put his arm around her, calming her, and guided her inside.

Jake kept riding, hard. So hard that he started to puff, and he was no longer cold; instead, the wind on his face felt deliciously cool. Something about the look on the woman's face made him feel uneasy, but at the same time he was glad he had seen her. He couldn't think why he found her so interesting. She looked so young and smooth next to the stooped and wrinkled old man, and she didn't seem so crazy today, just upset.

He biked until he couldn't breathe, then threw the bike on the ground and jogged to the nearest rocks. He lay down on one, like a seal, and waited until his heart slowed down and his breathing no longer hurt his chest. From where he lay on his stomach, Jake could see the slit in the rocks where the sealskin had been hidden. He kept very still, looking at it, and as he did so, he spotted a movement. The crevice was maybe ten metres away, and a small brown shape was moving towards it. Jake held his breath a moment, willing the seal not to see him. It was much smaller than those he'd seen throwing themselves into the water. It was practically a baby. It pulled itself along the rock, grunting slightly, almost as if it were humming a tune to itself the way Jake liked to do as he walked. It stopped every now and then and sniffed the air, but Jake was to the north, so his scent would be carried away by the breeze. Finally the seal reached the narrow cave, took one last look around and disappeared inside it.

Jake watched with anticipation, and waited a minute, maybe two. He thought about creeping up to the cave, looking in, maybe even trying to make friends with the young seal. Maybe he could pat it. He wished he could talk to it, communicate with it somehow. But as he started to move towards it he knew he was being silly. It was a wild animal. There was no way it would want to be his pet. He stopped and retreated to his lookout.

Soon the seal came out. It was quivering, suddenly nervous — scared even. It looked around and caught sight of Jake and before Jake could do anything, it had bounded across the rocks and dived into the water. Jake jumped up and tried to find the animal among the surging masses of seaweed, but it must have dived and kept on swimming. He was just about to turn away when he caught sight of its shining head. It had popped up, quite close, and its black eyes glistened as it stared at him. It must have felt safer in the sea. Even when Jake stole up to the edge of the water, it didn't swim away. It was watching him.

'Hi, little fella.' He crouched down and stretched a hand out towards it.

The seal bobbed around in the surf. It

bobbed closer. Jake got down onto his knees and reached down towards it. It bobbed so close that if he just reached out a little bit further, he could maybe . . .

Jake gasped as he came up for air from the sting of the cold water. He hadn't even felt himself slipping, he had been so intent on touching the stupid seal. Luckily, he was a good swimmer and the sea wasn't too rough today. He'd seen it on other days, beating itself against the rocks — to be caught in the ocean on a day like that would mean being bashed around for sure. He looked around but the seal was gone. He swam to the rocks and pulled himself back up, where he lay, shivering and wet. He heard a chattering sound. When he looked up the seal was close by again. This time Jake was sure it was laughing at him. Then, with a flick of its back flippers, it dived under and disappeared.

4

Jake tried to move quickly but the wind cut through his wet clothes, making his muscles cold and stiff. I'll freeze to death before I make it home, he thought, and imagined himself curling up inside the cave to shelter, falling asleep and never waking up. Nobody would ever find him except the seals, snuffling around his body, poking their whiskers in his ears.

He managed to climb back onto his bike

and get his feet to turn the pedals. Once he was moving, he didn't feel the cold so much. He could see the old man standing outside the shack, looking down the road at him. He had an urge to get off his bike and go and hide, but he pushed on, not wanting to let the cold catch up with him.

'Hey, young fella,' called the man as Jake passed. 'Stop!' For a moment Jake pretended not to hear him, but when the old man called out again, he put his foot down and skidded to a stop.

'Come here, you silly lad.'

Jake turned his bike around and pedalled back.

'Just look at you! Did you fall in the water, or what?'

Jake hung his head and nodded. 'I tried to touch a seal. I fell in.'

'You tried to . . .' The old man let out a great guffaw, showing Jake the pink insides of his mouth and yellow teeth. 'Why aren't I surprised? You've got to watch those seals, cheeky sods.

They'll have your arm off if you're not careful.'

Jake shrugged and turned to go. The man put a hand on his shoulder.

'Now just wait, young fella,' said the man. 'I'm only teasing. You can't go home like that, you'll freeze your backside off. Come inside by the fire and I'll give you something to wear.' He saw Jake eyeing up his own dirty jumper and pants. 'Don't worry, I've got some freshly washed clothes in here, although God knows I'm running low. I never seem to have enough these days.'

Jake was so cold, and the idea of a nice fire and dry clothes certainly appealed to him. And a part of him was curious to see the red-haired young woman, meet her properly, even. His mother's voice in his head told him not to go into a stranger's house, but he wanted to see what it was like inside, so he pushed the voice aside and followed the man into the shack.

'What's your name?' the old man asked.

'Jake.'

'Pleased to meet you, Jake. I saw you yesterday too, didn't I? You like it out here? I'm Ted. You want a cuppa?'

Jake shook his head and looked around the cottage. It only had one room. The young woman was nowhere to be seen, which was disappointing, though he couldn't think why. In one corner stood a single bed with a patchwork quilt and a thin pillow; in the opposite corner a pot-bellied stove crackled away.

'Well, here you go. I'll just be outside.' Ted handed Jake a pile of clothes and turned away. When he was gone, Jake brought the clothes to his face to give them a sniff. They smelt of laundry powder and a faint tang of sea air.

They were too big, of course, but the coarse pants had a piece of rope through the belt loops to hold them up, and he rolled the cuffs up. He folded up the sleeves of the shirt, feeling ridiculous. There was no way he could ride home like this, but already he was feeling much warmer without the wet clothes next to his skin. He draped his jeans, hoodie, T-shirt and socks over two chairs by the stove.

A voice came from outside. 'Ya decent?'

'Yes!' said Jake.

Ted limped back inside. 'It's like Grand Central Station in here today. Never had so many visitors.'

Jake thought of the red-haired woman, but was too shy to ask about her.

Ted went to a makeshift kitchen bench and opened a biscuit tin. He held it out. Jake expected to see something home-made, some crazy cake that if he ate it would make him grow as tall as a house, or maybe shrink down to the size of a garden gnome. But the tin contained only gingernuts, shop-bought ones. He took one with relief and a little bit of disappointment. This old man was turning out to be less strange than he had feared, but he realised he wanted him to be strange as well. It would give him something to tell his two best friends when he went back to school in a couple of weeks.

Jake was sitting in an old armchair, willing his clothes to dry faster, when there was a commotion at the back door, like the clattering of tin cans.

'Is it you?' Ted called suddenly. Jake jumped. In answer, the tins clattered again. 'Well come in, then, we have a visitor but he won't bite.' Ted winked at Jake with a wonky eye.

At first nobody came, but then a small hand appeared on the door frame, followed piece by piece by a small body. A little girl's face peeked around the corner. She had red-brown hair, like the woman in the overcoat, but she was no more than ten years old. She looked at him with curiosity. Her eyes were huge in her face, almost black. Then she giggled and disappeared.

'Ah, she's a shy one, that one,' said Ted. 'Cheeky too, as you've seen.' He coughed. '*Can* see.'

'Who is she?' asked Jake.

'Oh, she's . . .' Ted trailed off, thinking for a moment. 'She's my granddaughter. So she is.' He seemed to be surprised, as if he'd only just remembered that he had one. 'She stays with me sometimes. I can't keep track of how fast she's growing, though. Seems like yesterday she was a tiny baby.'

Ted went to the door and looked out. 'No, she's gone. Off to play on the rocks, no doubt. I know she'd like to meet you. Why don't you come back tomorrow. I'll make sure she's here to stay this time.'

'Well . . .' Jake wasn't sure. But the little girl had piqued his curiosity. The way she looked at him made him want to talk to her, to find out what was going on behind those dark eyes. She was younger than him, so maybe they wouldn't have much to say to each other, but maybe if she was cheeky, like Ted said, she could be fun to hang out with. He hadn't met any kids his own age here.

'Now,' said Ted, clapping his hands. 'I've got things to do. Do you want to wear my clothes home and bring 'em back tomorrow, or do want to put yours back on?'

Jake wondered what on earth the things were that Ted had to do. Drink some more tea, maybe. A whole lot of crossword puzzle books were piled up on the table next to his chair. Perhaps that was keeping him busy. He wondered how the old man ate. He didn't seem to have a car and he was miles from the shops. Suddenly Jake felt sorry for him. He was too thin — his clothes hung off him and his face was just a mass of sharp angles and loose skin. The eyelid of his squinty eye seemed thick and too heavy.

'Do you want me to bring you anything tomorrow?'

The old man looked thrown for a moment. Jake thought he saw a tear welling in his good eye.

'Well, that's very thoughtful of you, young sir. If you could go to the shops for me and buy some vegetables, maybe, I'd thank you. I've got some money here, somewhere.' He dug around inside his pockets but they came up empty. 'Could you check yours?'

Jake put his hand in the pocket of the pants he was wearing and found a piece of paper. A folded-up ten-dollar note that had gone through the wash.

'I knew I'd put it somewhere like that!' said Ted. 'You know, I get plenty of fish to eat, and I do have a couple of young helpers, but, as you saw with my young granddaughter there, they are not always reliable. So yes, thank you. Some veges I can boil and call my own would be fine.'

As Jake cycled away in his own clothes, still slightly damp, with the ten-dollar note snug in his pocket, he felt very good about himself. The old man might be strange, but he also seemed rather lonely as well. Jake was proud that he could be of some help. Then he remembered, with a stab of guilt, that he had been of no help to the poor dog. He only hoped he didn't bump into the bully boys on his way home and that the Labrador was unharmed, no thanks to him.

5

The boys were gone when he reached the blue and white house with the whirling windmills. The front door was open, and classical music wafted from inside. Perhaps he should go and ring the doorbell and see if the dog was all right. But then he'd have to admit that he hadn't stopped the bullies from tormenting the poor animal. He blushed at the memory, and his legs just wouldn't let him walk through the gate. As he turned to go, the dog came trotting outside with a bone. Its tail was wagging. Jake nearly shouted with joy, but instead he pedalled quietly away.

When he got home, Dad was sitting drinking tea at the table.

'There you are,' he said. 'How's your day been?'

Eager to forget the incident with the dog, Jake told him about what had happened at the beach, about falling in the water, and offering to help the old man.

'I don't know if I'm very happy about this, Jake,' said his dad.

'But I thought you'd be proud of me,' said Jake. He felt his face growing hot. When he was younger, he would have started crying; now he just felt angry.

'I *am* proud of you.' Dad pulled him in for a quick hug. His face was scratchy as usual, even though he shaved every day. He pushed Jake away and looked deep into his eyes, pinning his arms to his sides. 'But going into a stranger's house. Changing your clothes . . . I'm beginning to feel like a bad parent. I think I've let you have too much freedom.'

'No!' Jake turned away. 'I like my freedom. You're too busy to do anything with me anyway.' What would he do, cooped up in the house where his dad could see him all day?

'I just want you to be more responsible, mate. But it's not your fault; it's mine. Maybe you're too young to be off on your own like that.'

'I'm not!' Jake exploded. He thought his ears would burst. He didn't want to talk about it any more. He stomped off to his room, shutting — not slamming — the door behind him.

His father followed him in and sat on the bed, where Jake lay with his face in his pillow.

'Okay,' said his dad. 'We need to talk about this. We need to sort it out. I think it's great that you offered to help this old guy out, Jake — that's really kind of you. That makes me feel like your mum and me have done something right in bringing you up. Maybe I overreacted. But please, please don't go wandering off into strangers' houses. Surely you remember that's the first lesson we taught you when you were little — don't talk to strangers, no matter how many biscuits they offer you.'

Jake nodded. He lifted his face from his pillow. 'I know all that. But I was wet and cold. I didn't want to get pneumonia and die. You wouldn't want that, would you?'

His dad chuckled. 'No, of course not. But that's the other thing. How can I rest easy knowing you're throwing yourself into freezing cold water? You could have drowned. The sea gets so rough out there, mate. You need to think about what you've done. No Red Rocks for you tomorrow while I think about what to do with you.'

'Aw, Dad!'

'No "aw, Dads" thank you.'

'But —'

'No buts either.'

After Dad left the room, Jake rolled onto his back and fingered the ten-dollar note in his pocket. He had wanted to remind his dad that he had it, but couldn't get a word in edgeways. What was he supposed to do with it? He'd wait and see what his father said tomorrow, then find some way to get it back to Ted. He hung his head over the side of the bed and peered into the darkness. The sealskin was still there, waiting.

The next day dragged. Jake stayed in bed reading a book long after breakfast while his dad worked in his writing shed. After lunch, he asked if he could go down to the beach in front of the house.

'Not too far,' said Dad. 'I want to be able to see you.'

The narrow, rocky foreshore was deserted, apart from a huge crowd of black-backed gulls who were hanging about on a patch of sand. They looked as though they were having a well-behaved party. Jake picked up a stick and drew monster faces and spaceships in the sand between the black rocks. When he got bored with that he tried to see how many times he could break the stick in half. It only took three times before the bits got too small to break. He threw the pieces, one by one, into the sea, which was calm today, quietly sluicing the coarse sand with tiny frilly waves. He turned to look back up to where his dad sat, at his desk in the shed. He could see a dark shape, so he waved, but there was no movement. Perhaps he wasn't watching after all. Jake thought about taking off — not to Red Rocks, but maybe just to the shop, to get an ice cream. He still had the ten-dollar note in his pocket.

Just as he was about to start out for the dairy, he saw a figure coming along the road towards him. It walked on the footpath, but kept stopping every few metres. Jake waited, intrigued. It wasn't long before he saw it was the red-haired woman. She was pausing at each letterbox and staring hard at each house for a few seconds before moving on, still looking as though she was searching for something. Her grey coat flapped about her knees. Jake crouched down behind the bank that led up to the road. He waited. He imagined her stopping at his dad's letterbox, then looking up at him working away on his book. Jake wondered if his dad had seen her or if he was too engrossed in his work. He was about to pop up and see if the woman had passed by when he heard the sound of a window being flung open.

'*Jake!*' There was real anxiety in his father's voice. Jake stood up, glad now that he hadn't taken off to the shop, ice cream or no. He climbed up the bank, back onto the road. The woman was nowhere to be seen.

'I'm here,' he called, and waved with both arms over his head.

Dad beckoned, and Jake went back through the front gate and up the path at the side of the house.

His father's writing shed was smaller

than Jake's bedroom. An armchair sat in one corner, and a desk by the window. The walls were covered with pictures of sea birds and marine life: whales, jellyfish, sharks. It was quiet today, but on stormy days the hut rattled and whistled.

On one wall there was a picture of some baby seals — the cute kind, the ones that get killed for their white fur. It reminded Jake of what he had under his bed, and he wondered again who had left it, who could have been so cruel as to skin a seal. Or perhaps the seal had already died before its coat was taken. He thought again about telling his father about it, but stopped himself. Dad would want to put it back, or worse, keep it for himself. He felt a flash of anger, then surprise that the sealskin had stirred such strong feelings in him, as if it had some magic pull over him.

'You okay?' asked Dad.

'Yes,' said Jake, but he knew he didn't sound okay.

'Really? What have you been up to?'

Jake shrugged, then dropped himself into the armchair.

'How about we go for a ride in the boat soon? Maybe tomorrow or the next day, if the weather's good.'

Jake shrugged again. 'Sure.' The truth was that he was excited by the idea of going out in the boat, but he wanted his dad to feel a little bit guilty for not letting him roam free. It seemed to be working, too.

Then he remembered the woman with the red hair. 'Did you see that crazy lady again?'

'You mean the one from the fish and chip shop? Don't say "crazy" like that, Jake, it's mean. And no, where was she?'

'She was walking along the road, looking at all the houses.'

Dad frowned. 'Really? That's strange. You see why I don't like you wandering around. Where did she go?'

Jake wished now he hadn't said anything.

'I don't know. She was there one minute, then she was gone.'

Dad threw a screwed-up piece of paper at him and smiled, suddenly twinkly. 'You sure she wasn't a ghost? Sure you didn't make her up?'

'Ha ha,' said Jake, still not smiling, but he wondered for a moment if maybe he had imagined her — after all, she had just disappeared, and his mum and teachers always told him he had an overactive imagination, that he was too dreamy.

Jake's dad must have felt really guilty, because that afternoon he finished work early and took Jake to the movies in Island Bay. Afterwards they went to an Indian restaurant for dinner, and Jake had his favourite, butter chicken, which was creamy and delicious, and not too spicy. His dad dared him to eat some of his vindaloo, and he couldn't say no, but afterwards his tongue tingled with a fire that no amount of water could put out.

When the meal was finished and his dad got up to pay, he turned to Jake and said, 'I've come to a decision, Jake. You can keep going to Red Rocks, but I want to meet this Ted character. We'll buy the veges and I'll come with you tomorrow to help deliver them, okay?'

Jake nodded. Things were going to be just fine.

6

Ten dollars didn't buy a lot of vegetables, but Jake's dad topped up the bag with a few extras — some crisp apples and some bright spinach on top of the carrots, onions, broccoli and potatoes — even though Jake guessed he probably couldn't afford it.

They walked without talking, Jake trotting ahead and looking back as his father's feet crunched steadily on the stones. Soon, the shack, with its grey, peeling paint, came into view. The air carried the smell of smoke from the wood stove. Jake suddenly felt nervous about the coming meeting, but he wasn't sure whether he didn't want Ted to meet his dad or the other way around. As they approached the front door, he walked very close behind Dad, just as he'd done when he was small, ready to hide behind him if needed.

Ted took a long time to answer the door. He looked tired, as though he had just woken from a nap. Jake noticed for the first time that he had patches of grey hair sprouting from his cheeks, well above his beard, and his skin was cracked like a dry riverbed. His bad eye was nearly closed.

'Ted, is it?' said Dad, and held out the bag of vegetables. 'We've got a delivery for you.'

Ted nodded, took the bag and limped inside, leaving the door open. Dad stuck his head inside. 'Should we come in?' he said.

'Please yourself,' said Ted.

This was not going how Jake had hoped. If Ted was rude and horrible, there was surely no way his dad would let him play out here any more. They stepped inside. Maybe Ted was angry with him for taking two days to come back. He wondered if he should apologise, but his shyness had cemented his mouth shut.

Ted had limped his way to the kitchen bench, and in the corner, crouching on the single bed, was the little girl from the other day. She looked like a scared animal, with her legs pulled up inside the oversized jersey she wore. Grubby bare feet poked out from under it.

'This is my granddaughter, Jessie,' said Ted.

As soon as he said it, Dad's hand, which had been holding tightly to Jake's shoulder, relaxed.

'Pleased to meet you, Jessie,' said his dad. 'I'm Robert. This is Jake.' He squeezed Jake's shoulder.

'We've met,' said Jake.

'Oh?' said Dad. 'You never said.'

Jake didn't say anything.

'Sit down, sit down,' said Ted. 'Tea's made.'

Dad pushed Jake towards the single bed and sat himself down in one of the two armchairs. Jake perched on the end of the bed as far from Jessie as he could get. He felt the girl staring at him, but when he looked at her she looked away. He studied her profile for a moment. She had a pointy, upturned nose and her hair was the colour of rust.

Dad asked Ted if he did much fishing, and pretty soon the adults were in deep conversation about what was the best kind of rod and bait to use, whether it was best to cast into the surf or go out in a boat. Jake stopped listening when he realised that Jessie was playing a game with him, trying to get him to catch her staring at him, even poking her tongue out at him. Soon she couldn't stop herself from giggling and he had a grin on his face as well.

It was only when the grown-ups started talking about the seals that Jessie stopped playing the game and started listening, so Jake did too.

'But they're all bachelors, those seals,' his dad was saying. 'They come over from the top of the South Island when they don't have a mate and wait out the breeding season.'

'Ah, don't believe everything you've heard,' said Ted. 'I've seen the odd female there; juveniles, too.'

'Are you sure they're not just small males you've seen?'

'Nah. I'm not stupid. I know what to look for. The females are smaller in the neck. They carry their fat lower down.'

'I'm sorry, sir.' Dad was polite suddenly, as if afraid he'd offended Ted. 'Well, that's fascinating. I've been thinking about writing a book about the wildlife on Wellington's south coast, actually. The seals would be a good place to start. I reckon plenty of people would buy a book like that.'

Ted looked at Jessie, who was staring at the old man, her dark eyes narrowed.

'Ah . . .' He was still looking at Jessie. 'What

about the penguins? They're much more interesting. Did you know that the little blue penguin . . .'

Jessie smiled and moved suddenly. Her legs shot out the bottom of her jumper, showing raggedy cut-off shorts, and she jumped down to the floor. 'Come on,' she said, and took Jake's hand. She pulled him to his feet.

Jake's dad stopped talking mid-sentence and smiled. 'Yes, go, go. I'm fine here with Ted. Go and play, by all means.' This was a good sign, that Dad liked Ted.

'Aren't you cold?' asked Jake when they got outside. The wind was not as icy as it had been the other day; it blew from the north, much more gently, but it was still wintry.

'No,' said Jessie. 'Let us go down to the water.'

Her voice sounded strange, as though she had a foreign accent, but Jake couldn't place it. She spoke too slowly and her voice was deep for a girl. She walked into the sea and stood with the water lapping at her knees.

'I'm not going in there again,' he said. 'I fell in the other day and it was freezing.'

Jessie's face broke into a smile. She laughed, a weird barking sound. 'I know.' She stopped laughing suddenly. 'I mean, my grandfather told me.'

Jake sat down on a log and started biffing stones into the water. Jessie, who had been so quiet, now started asking him a lot of questions. Like, where did he live? Did he have any brothers and sisters? Did he go to school? (Of course he did! What a silly question.)

'What about you?' Jake asked. 'Where do you normally live?'

Jessie stood up from where she had been trailing her hands in the water. She didn't seem to care how wet she got. 'Over there.' She pointed out to sea. On clear days you could see the snowy mountains of the South Island, but not today.

'Over the water, you mean?' asked Jake. Jessie nodded.

'In Picton?'

She hesitated then said, 'Yes.'

'Did you come over on the ferry?'

'Yes.' Then she sat, fully clothed, in the water and started pouring it over herself with her hands, as if she were taking a warm bath. 'I live in a big house with my father and my mother. I have ten brothers and ten sisters. I go to school every single day. Except for when I am staying here with my grandfather.'

She's lying, thought Jake. Oh well, let her make up stories. He didn't really care. There was one thing he wanted to know though.

'Who's that red-haired woman I saw here the other day?'

Jessie stopped playing with the water and stared at him. 'She is my aunt.'

'So she's Ted's daughter?'

She thought for a moment. 'Yes.'

'What's her name?'

Again, Jessie hesitated. 'Cara . . . Cara . . . Caraway.'

Jake started to get annoyed. How could he be sure she was telling the truth? Caraway wasn't even a name. He was pretty sure it was a kind of spice.

'Well, what's she looking for, then?'

Jessie stood up. She came walking out of the water towards him. Her skin had turned a light shade of blue, but she wasn't shivering. 'What do you mean?' she asked. She looked scared.

'I keep seeing her everywhere. She just walks around looking in windows and people's front yards and everything. Dad thinks she's not right in the head.'

'Not right in the head? What does this mean?'

'You know.' Jake tapped his temple with his finger. 'Crazy.'

He thought he might make her mad, and he regretted it as soon as he said it. But she just sighed and sat down on the log beside him.

'It is complicated,' she said. 'You would not understand.'

Her shoulder was touching his. The cold and wetness soaked into his hoodie. He felt a shiver go down his body and knew that he couldn't ask her any more.

'Come on,' he said. 'Let's go back inside. Dad's probably waiting for me.'

But when they got back to Ted's hut, his dad looked very comfortable, with a fresh mug of tea in his hand. He didn't seem impatient at all, even though he'd warned Jake on the way over that he had a lot of work he needed to do that day.

'Jake! Jessie!' Dad beamed at them. It was as though he was drunk. Then Jake saw why.

Sitting on the bed, opposite Dad, was Caraway. Despite her shabby, too-big clothes, she managed to look graceful as she crossed her long, bare legs. Jake felt himself blushing and looked away.

'This is my son, Jake,' said Dad. 'My pride and joy.'

Jake wished his father would shut up; he was

embarrassing him now, making him feel like a little kid. He didn't want to be a little kid in front of Caraway.

'Jake, this is —'

'Caraway,' said Jake. 'I know. Hi.'

Dad let out a guffaw, and the woman smiled. 'Caraway!' said Dad. 'Like the spice? Oh Jake, that's hilarious. Where on earth did you get that idea?'

Jake looked around for Jessie, but the front door was open. She had scarpered. He balled his fists and stared at the ground.

'It is Cara,' said the woman, standing up and coming towards him. 'Just Cara.' She reached out a hand and Jake took it. Her fingers were smooth and cool and slightly damp. She didn't seem at all crazy any more, and the sadness and worry he had seen before were gone. Her dark eyes looked straight into his and he found himself staring. The rest of the room appeared to go dark around them. A light breeze came from somewhere, and the sound of sea intensified.

There was something about her that he couldn't place, and something was happening to him that he couldn't control. The sea seemed to know it, and the wind, and the cliffs behind the house, which stretched and leaned in and moaned . . .

'You can let go of her hand now, Jake,' said Dad.

Jake dropped it, and the room was ordinary again. His father was grinning at him foolishly and Jake blushed again. Why was Dad determined to embarrass him?

'Where's Ted?' he asked.

'He's outside,' said Dad. 'Chopping wood. I offered to do it for him, but he wouldn't let me. I thought I'd better keep Cara here company anyway.' He smiled a gooey smile at her.

Yuck, thought Jake. He's gone all moon-eyed over her, like his friends were over Sarah, a girl at school. He supposed Sarah was quite pretty, but she was young and silly. Not like Cara.

Suddenly he had the urge to get Dad as far away from Cara as he could.

'Can we go?' he said. 'You said you had work to do.'

'Yes . . . yes, so I do.' His father rose reluctantly to his feet. 'It was delightful to meet you . . . Cara.'

She just nodded at him. But she winked at Jake. It didn't matter how grey and worn her clothes were; in the dark little shack, she shone like the sun.

7

The next few days were sunny and unusually warm for the end of winter, and Jake could feel the end of the holidays approaching. He had talked to his mum on the phone a few times. She said she missed him and that she couldn't wait for him to get home, but the last time she had said that, he'd returned to find his bedroom had been turned into the baby's room. He'd had to move downstairs. Mum and Greg had acted like it was a big adventure, but the new room was cold and he felt far away from everybody on stormy nights. With any luck, there'd be no new surprises when he got home this time.

His father had relaxed a bit now that he had met Ted and Cara properly. He acted eager to get Jake out of the house some mornings, supposedly because he had to work, but sometimes when Jake arrived home he could see his dad up in his workroom, just staring out to sea in a daze.

Jake and Jessie had become good friends, despite her strange ways: that weird voice and the dark eyes that he would find watching him all the time. Something else was odd. When he first met her, he had thought she was much younger than him, but now, less than a week later, she seemed the same age. Maybe he was just used to her company, but he was sure that she was taller as well, nearly as tall as he was.

They explored rock pools for hours and collected the shells that lay bleached and empty amongst the stones of the beach. He brought a pack of cards with him and taught her how to play poker, using the shells as currency. She had never played with a deck of cards before, and Jake had to keep reminding her which cards were the spades, and which were the diamonds.

There was no sign of Cara, and Jake didn't ask after her. He supposed that she lived somewhere else — after all, there wouldn't be any room for her to sleep at Ted's house. He thought he saw her one day, in the distance, still wandering around the streets, but he couldn't be sure. She appeared in his dreams some nights, and Jake always woke up feeling hot and embarrassed afterwards.

He stayed away from Ted. Even though his father had given him the nod of approval, Jake still found the old man a bit weird, mainly because he constantly talked to himself. Often Jake would turn up at the shack on his bike and neither Ted nor Jessie would be home. But if he called out, Jessie would come gliding towards him over the rocks, wet as if from a swim, smelling of salt and seaweed. Ted would appear as a silhouette out to sea, bobbing about in his dinghy, where he sat patiently for half the day, only coming in when he had a catch of fish. Jessie would bump up against him as he brought the bucket into the house, eagerly straining to catch a glimpse of what was inside. Ted had to smack her hands away.

'Easy, girl!' he'd say. 'We've got company. Let's get these into the frying pan and then we'll eat them, eh?'

The three of them would sit around, eating whole cooked fish off blue-rimmed metal plates balanced on their laps. Ted showed Jake how to lift the meat from the bones, then turn the fish over and prise the skeleton away. Jessie concentrated hard on her lunch, sucking every last piece of meat from the bones, even the eyes! Afterwards she didn't seem to notice when she had fish smeared on her cheeks and in her hair; she just walked around with a small smile on her face, looking satisfied.

After one such lunch, Jake told Jessie they should walk to Red Rocks to look at the seals.

'Let us not,' she said. 'I like it here, with you.'

'But I'm coming, too! Come on, it'll be fun. One of them nearly let me touch it the other day.' He didn't mention the fact that that was when he fell in the water.

'Oh, you want to go for another swim, do you?' Jessie laughed. 'Anyway, you should not get too close. Some of the seals are nice, but some of them are mean.'

'I know.' She could be such a little know-it-all sometimes, talking to him as if she was a grown-up and he was a bit stupid.

He ignored her and started walking towards the rocks without looking back. He could feel those dark eyes on his back, until she relented and scrabbled after him, her feet so tough that she barely flinched as they marched over the stony path. He could smell the seals before he got to them. The whole air was thick with their stink. A couple of thick-necked large ones were lying in the sun, lifting their pointy noses only to yawn, their whiskers sparkling in the light. They opened an eye each and watched as Jake crept closer and closer. Jake didn't know why he was getting so close. He wanted to prove something to Jessie, but what? To show he was brave.

'Jake,' she pleaded. 'Please come back. They do not like it.'

As if in answer, one of the seals lifted its head and growled at him, like a dog. He stopped where he was, suddenly frightened, but when he tried to step back without taking his eyes off it, his foot missed a step and he stumbled backwards.

Then, out of nowhere, another seal appeared from behind the larger ones. It lumbered towards Jake, fat neck outstretched and mouth open. Its gums flashed, bright pink. Jake screamed and put his hands over his head, desperately trying to scramble his way back across the loose rock. He felt the skin on his calf scraping off through his torn jeans. He wasn't sure what happened next, but it was as if a great wind picked him up and spun him away. Jessie had thrown him like an empty sack and she now stood between Jake and the seal, crouched low. A low, inhuman growl emanated from her body. The seal stopped. It was smaller than the other two, who looked on with passive interest, but it was still bigger than Jessie. Jake was frozen to the spot, waiting to see what happened. If Jessie was attacked, he would never forgive himself.

'Jessie —' he called out to her, but his voice was weak and barely audible over the waves that now hurled themselves against the rocks.

Jessie and the seal stared at each other for what felt to Jake like a full minute. Then the seal shook its head, rose up and turned its back. It flopped away across the rock and dived into the water. The two larger seals went back to their nap as if nothing had happened.

Jake's heart was still beating fast as he got to his feet. Jessie spun around at the sound his shoes made on the small stones. The sight of her made him take a step back. Her irises had grown huge and black, and the way she was crouched, with her small pointed teeth bared and her hair blowing in the wind, reminded him once again of an animal.

'Hey,' said Jake. 'It's only me.'

Jessie covered her face with her hands for a moment and took a deep breath. Her fingers were spread wide, and Jake caught a glimpse of taut blue skin between them.

She took her hands away and when she looked up at him again, the whites of her eyes had returned and she was just a little girl again.

'What on earth was that?' he asked, still incredulous that she had been so brave and had successfully scared the seal off.

Jessie straightened up and walked past him, jumping from the rock down onto the beach. 'I told you to stay away. You would not listen. You could have been killed, you know.' Her voice was remarkably calm.

Jake followed her. 'So could you!' he said.

'Yes,' was all she said. 'Come on, let us go.'

'Wait.' Jake grabbed her arm. 'I want to show you something. You know about seals. Come and tell me what you think about this.'

They walked further, keeping an eye out for any more seals. But the rocks were bare. A few heads bobbed in amongst the shining kelp and the swell of the waves. They came to the rock with the crevice in it. Jessie looked unsurprised, as if she knew it was there.

'Look,' said Jake. 'It's a cave. It just looks like a slit in the rocks, but when you go in it opens out.'

'I can see that.' She still sounded annoyed with him, and seemed impatient to leave. She stood with both her hands on her hips.

'Come on,' said Jake. 'I'll show you.' He moved towards the crevice and started to crouch down, ready to crawl in.

'No, don't.' Jessie stopped him with a hand on his arm. 'You don't know what might be in there.'

He was inclined to listen to her this time. Did she know about the sealskin? Could he trust her with his secret? There was only one way to find out. 'I found something in there once. It was so cool. I don't know how it got in there, though. Maybe you do, since you know about the seals.'

A frown creased her forehead as she waited for him to go on.

'I found a sealskin.'

Jessie gasped, and looked more fearful than when she had confronted the seal.

'It's okay,' he said quickly. 'It wasn't bloody, or anything.'

'What did you do with it?' she asked.

'I took it home. It was heavy.'

Jessie sat down on the rocks with a bump. 'But Jake, you must not take it home. You must put it back!'

'But why?' asked Jake. 'Do you know how it got there?'

Jessie looked around, uncomfortable. She

scratched her head as if buying time. Jake waited.

'Do you know what a selkie is?' she asked.

'A selkie? No. Should I?'

'Selkies are seal-people. The seals come on land and they shed their skins so they can walk the earth like humans do. When they have finished their business, they put their skins back on and become seals again.'

'But that's just a fairy story,' said Jake, who could now remember something he had heard a long time ago. A story, set in Ireland maybe, where his ancestors had come from.

Jessie stared at him, hard. 'It is not a story. It is real. Jake, if you have stolen a sealskin, then whoever it belongs to will be stuck in human form.' Jake was surprised to see tears form in her eyes. 'You must put it back.'

'But that's the stupidest thing I've ever heard!' said Jake.

'Jake!' Jessie shouted. 'You must put it back.'

What did she know? She was being ridiculous, a baby, and he told her so.

Sobbing now, Jessie stood up and ran away from him, disappearing into the rocks.

Jake stood still, wondering whether to follow her or not, to comfort her, tell her he was sorry. But he was a little frightened of her. If she was upset, he didn't want to provoke her any more, to see that wild, dark-eyed face again. Instead, he decided to wait for her to calm down and come back. In the meantime, he would explore the crevice once more.

The rocks were sharp on his knees, and the scrapes on his legs from his encounter with the seal were aching. It was dark inside the cave. He waited for his eyes to adjust before moving forward. A thin musky smell, like the seals but fainter, hung about the air. He shuffled forward with his hands in front and once again, his fingers came in contact with fur. This time, he didn't shout, but he pulled sharply away and backed out of the cave, then ran away as fast as he could.

8

The air was different when Jake got home. He felt it as the front door swung open. It was thicker, harder to breathe. He heard a murmuring coming from the living room, and was about to push open the door to investigate when he remembered his torn jeans. The last thing he wanted to do was explain to his father that he had been rescued from a seal attack by a little girl, let alone tell him about the fight he'd had with Jessie about the sealskin. He ducked instead into his room and changed into trackpants, pulling them carefully over his scraped and bloodied calf. He'd clean himself later, in the shower. In his socks, he walked silently down the hall and opened the living room door.

His father looked up sharply and a flash passed over his face — fear? No, it was the same look he'd worn when he'd told Jake he was moving out of their home. *Guilt*. But this time, it was gone as quickly as it had arrived.

The room smelled of coffee and sea air; Jake filled his lungs with it. He recognised the deep red hair before Cara turned around and gave him a penetrating stare. He expected her to smile at him, but she didn't — she just stared, as if he were a bug under a microscope that she was about to dissect. He remembered the strange effect she'd had on him in Ted's shack, but this time the wind and sea stayed where they belonged.

'Jake,' said his dad. 'I wasn't expecting you back so soon. What's the time?'

'It's about four,' said Jake.

'Four?' Dad's eyes widened. 'I can't believe it! Where's the day gone?' He laughed, nervously Jake thought, and looked at Cara, whose gaze was still fixed on Jake. 'Lots to talk about I suppose.'

Jake looked at the ground, unable to stand the intensity of Cara's stare, and she finally turned back. 'Perhaps I should leave,' she said.

'Yes, I suppose.' Dad looked forlorn. They both stood, Cara unfolding her long body. She was nearly as tall as Dad was. Jake looked at her feet, which were filthy. Why didn't she put some shoes on? What was wrong with her? As they passed by him on the way to the front door, Cara brushed past him and his arm tingled. He snatched it away from her and rubbed it as if he'd been burnt. She turned her black eyes to him when she got to the door.

'Goodbye, Jake,' she said in a whisper, and

stepped outside. Jake's dad followed her, and pulled the front door almost shut behind him as he murmured something to her. Jake could see his fingers pressed into the door. He wanted to walk forward, to hear what they were saying to each other, but the sight of his father's hand on the door, the solid hunk of wood between them, made him feel unwanted, and he went into his room instead and shut the door.

Later, his father knocked softly.

'Jake? Dinner's ready.'

'I'm not hungry,' said Jake, although his stomach growled as he said it.

The door opened. 'What is it, mate?'

'Nothing.' Jake sat on his bed with his arms folded, his book dog-eared but unread beside him. He'd tried to read but he couldn't absorb the words.

Dad sat down next to him. He was quiet for a minute, staring at the floor, as if trying to decide what to say. Then he gave Jake a sideways shunt with his shoulder.

'Are you angry with me? About Cara?'

'No,' Jake said, but he didn't sound convinced. How could he explain how he was feeling when he didn't even know himself? He didn't like the fact that Dad had been alone with Cara. It couldn't be because he was jealous, could it? She was a grown-up; he was just a little kid. And yet he felt *something*, as if he had known her all his life and wanted to go on knowing her forever. It was insane, but Dad somehow felt like an impediment to knowing her. And yet. She scared him. She had the same dark, moody eyes as Jessie. He had seen what Jessie could do in a temper. Cara was older, and Jake just knew that the force inside her would be even stronger if provoked.

He said nothing of this to his father. He decided to shrug away his feelings, to pretend nothing was wrong for the sake of peace.

'I'm okay,' he said. He forced a smile. 'Maybe I'm hungry after all.'

'Great.' Jake heard the relief in his father's

voice. 'Because, Jake . . .' He stopped and sighed. 'You know since your mum and I broke up, there hasn't been anyone. And . . . you know, she has Greg, and now the baby, and maybe I'd like to find someone, too. You know? It can be a bit lonely by myself. When you're not here, of course,' he added quickly.

Jake didn't want to be having this conversation. He resisted the urge to stick his fingers in his ears.

'Yeah,' he said, and stood up. 'Whatever.'

He ate his dinner quickly, scared his dad would want to talk about Cara again. It was crazy. He'd only just met her, for goodness' sake. And he was talking about her like he wanted to settle down with her or something. Jake couldn't help wonder if this was why his dad had been so eager to get him out of the house in the mornings this week; if Cara had been visiting him every day. Maybe they were in love.

Oh, puke, thought Jake. He put his dinner

plate in the sink and, pleading a headache, went to bed early.

The next day, Jake woke up stiff and sore. His legs were scraped and bruised from where he had fallen on the rocks. He lay in the gloomy room and listened to the rain falling on the corrugated iron roof. It was usually a comforting sound, always reminding him of holidays with his father, since the roof in Auckland was made of tiles that made no sound. But it provided no comfort this morning, when he thought about his fight with Jessie and what his dad had tried to talk to him about last night.

He was relieved to be able to use the weather as an excuse not to visit Jessie. Instead, he moped around at home, eating toast and reading his book while his father worked. Jake almost felt as though his dad was avoiding him, but of course it was no different from his usual routine.

After a sombre lunch, and when Dad had

gone back to the shed, Jake sat looking out the window. The sea had turned brown from the rain, and the road was slick. The clouds hung low and moody over the bay. As he sat there looking, he became aware of a soft knocking sound, barely audible over the rain on the roof. Was there someone at the door? He waited to see if Dad appeared, but he didn't, and the tapping continued, like someone drumming their fingers along to a tune. He decided to go to the door, just to check.

When he opened it, he was surprised to see Jessie. She stood there looking very small and wet. Her bare arms seemed immune to the cold and she let the water from her hair stream into her eyes without wiping it away.

'Hi,' said Jake. 'What's up?' It didn't occur to him that she might visit him — he had always been the one to make the trip, although of course it wasn't just her that he went to see. It was the high cliffs and the glimpses of seals, the rock pools and the sad, windy beach.

'I missed you,' she said. 'Can I come in and play?'

He stood aside and let her in. She dripped puddles onto the wooden floor, so he handed her a towel to dry herself with. She looked at it, unsure what to do. He mimed drying his hair and she nodded and copied him. Then they stood awkwardly in the living room. Jessie looked around with interest and Jake saw the room through her eyes: it was small and untidy, with newspapers in messy piles on the couch and the floor, dirty coffee mugs on the table and cheap old curtains at the windows. It was so different from his home in Auckland, which had polished wooden floors that shone, and rich oriental rugs matched with red velvet curtains. His mother kept the place immaculate and he was scared to even leave his schoolbag on the floor. Here he could leave his dirty sneakers on the worn living room carpet and there still wouldn't be as much mess as his father made all by himself. He felt embarrassed suddenly, but then he remembered where Jessie was staying, and knew she wouldn't mind a bit of chaos.

'So, do you want to play cards, or . . .' He was waiting for her to say something about yesterday, about their fight, about how she had run away crying, but she just nodded and said, 'Yes.'

He beat her twice at Snap and the sense of unease didn't lift. It was strange having her in the house. She somehow didn't belong, so far from the rocks and the smell of salt and fish and the seals.

'Go again?' he asked.

'Can I look at your bedroom? Can we play there?'

Jake shrugged. 'Okay,' he said. Most of the toys in there were from when he was younger, cars and trains that he didn't take much interest in any more. He mostly just read books in there now.

As soon as Jessie entered the room, Jake, who was behind her, saw her shoulders stiffen.

She turned to one side with her face tilted up and he realised she was sniffing the air. Her pale face flushed.

'What's wrong?' he asked, but she said nothing and started pacing in a tight circle.

'Jessie . . .' He was about to tell her that she was freaking him out, to suggest they leave the room, when suddenly she dived to the floor and, with her fingernails scrabbling on the floorboards, disappeared under his bed. She let out an unearthly screech and emerged moments later with the sealskin clutched in her hands. Without stopping to think and giving her no warning, Jake stepped forward and ripped it from her hands.

'It's mine!' he shouted. 'Leave it alone!' Jessie moved towards him and to his surprise, he shoved her away. Jessie stared at him and her eyes took on the darkness he had seen yesterday. He hugged the sealskin to his chest, waiting for her to pounce on him, to fight him — a fight he would lose. But instead, she backed away, and tears welled in her eyes.

'You are no friend of mine,' she said. 'Or of the seals.' She ran from the house, out into the cold rain, slamming the door behind her.

Later that night, after the rain had abated, Jake took the sealskin from its new hiding place in his wardrobe. He still couldn't bring himself to show his father, because he knew he had done the wrong thing by taking it. He thought about what Jessie had told him about the selkies. Could it be true? He caught a glimpse of himself in the mirror, holding the skin. He stood up and went closer. He draped the skin around his shoulders, wrapping himself in it until it was hard to tell where the skin ended and Jake began. When he looked into the mirror again he got a fright — it was as if he had caught a glimpse of a live seal, standing upright in his room. He gave a small yelp and tore the skin off, throwing it on the floor.

'It's just a stupid story,' he said to himself

and got into bed, pulling the covers up around his ears to block out the sound of the sea pounding on the beach. He lay there, listening to his breath in the hot darkness, and tried not to think of Jessie.

9

Jake opened his eyes. It was still dark. He could hear the gentle shushing of the waves on the beach across the road. It was a constant noise, so he wasn't sure what had woken him, but in his dreams he had heard someone calling his name. He turned over and closed his eyes, trying to get back to sleep. Then he heard it again.

'*Jake.*' It was like a whisper, but it sounded

far away, so he shouldn't have been able to hear it. He sat up and held his breath to listen more intently. Maybe Dad was calling him, or talking in his sleep.

'*Jake.*' There it was again. It definitely wasn't coming from the direction of his father's room. It was coming from outside. Maybe Jessie was calling him, but he couldn't tell whether the voice was male or female, young or old. He flicked off the covers and went and stood by the window. He pushed it open. The sound of the waves grew louder, and floating on them came his name, drawn out, like a sigh: '*Jaaaake.*' And then: '*The skin. The skin.*'

His own skin prickled. He looked at the sealskin, which lay in a crumpled heap where he had recklessly left it before he went to bed. What if his father had come in and seen it? He picked it up, hugging its warmth to his body, and went back to the window. All he could see in the darkness was the weak moonlight on the sea. He pushed the window open further and dropped the skin on the ground outside. He pulled himself onto the sill then down onto the grass, close below. The grass tickled his feet and he shivered in his pyjamas. His name came again, and this time there was no mistaking: it came from the beach. He picked up the skin, crossed the silent road and found the track over the rocks down to the sand. Jake looked back at the house, but from where he stood, all that was visible was Dad's writing shed, and the windows were dark, blank eyes looking down at him.

'Jessie?' He called out, but the word was stolen from his lips by the wind. He shivered. Then another thought occurred to him.

'Cara?' It came out as barely a whisper. He walked down to the water. The moon was in the sky, but it was mostly hidden behind clouds, casting intermittent silver light on the rocky beach. He sat down on a log and cuddled the sealskin to himself to keep warm. Maybe he had dreamed the voice, or heard the wind catching on something, creating the eerie sound of his own name.

He looked out to sea. He had never been down here at night, and he took a moment to enjoy the strangeness of it. In the patches of light, he thought he made out seaweed in the surging water, and something else, floating out there, waiting. Seals! He stood up, and shivered in the wind. He heard it again: '*The skin. Jake.*' A row of seals, their wet heads dark against the sea, watched him, like a row of sentries guarding the sea. Or the beach.

He swallowed hard, but did not feel afraid. His bones were cold now, but his arms were warm where they held the seal's coat. He had an idea. He unfurled the sealskin and stepped inside it. Immediately he was flooded with heat, suddenly immune to the cold that had been licking at him. With the sealskin on his body, he felt as though it had melded with his own form. The sea beckoned and he longed to dive into it.

It was impossible to walk in the skin, so

he fell forward and landed on his flippers. He lumbered and jerked towards the water, moving like a seal. The water wasn't as icy as he had expected; the skin kept him warm and dry. He dived beneath the surface, and felt suddenly fast and free. He spun around as he dived, swimming with a grace and swiftness he had never before experienced. The water was so clear, it was as if he was wearing goggles. He held his breath for a long time and then emerged, laughing, into the air. He rolled onto his side and waved a flipper at the bobbing, silent heads, still watching him. Clouds moved across the moon and everything went dark.

Jake floated in the water, listening. All he could hear was the sound of the waves lapping the shore. He took a big breath and dived under again, feeling the velvet water slipping by him, the tickling of the kelp that floated in clumps near the surface. Above him, the moon must have emerged from the clouds: suddenly the water was filled with light and he became aware of shadows. He turned his head and saw dark shapes darting around him, coming closer and then veering away. He tried to chase after them, to play with them, but the seals were always just out of reach, just out of sight. He swam in circles, trying to catch a glimpse of them, until he was dizzy. He stopped, head spinning, and hung in the water and waited. Everything went dark again. Just as he was about to surface for another breath, he felt something brush by him. He spun to look at it and felt another body, pressing against him. Another bumped him from behind. Suddenly he was surrounded on all sides, and though he tried to kick with his back flippers, to rise out of the sea, the bodies around him kept him under the water. He felt hands pulling at him. Hands. *Human* hands. They pulled at his skin, tugging; it gave way and the icy water rushed in, surrounding his body, which now felt weak and small when only moments before he'd felt invincible. Jake gasped and took in a lungful of water, which hurt more than he could have imagined. He managed to struggle free for a moment, just enough to break for the surface and cough the water out of his lungs before he was pulled under again. He felt the last of the sealskin being ripped away from his body and as the moon came out again, he saw a woman's shape above him in the water, her bright hair cascading around her head, the sealskin in her hand. Then he gave up and closed his eyes, letting the sea take him.

Moments later, he felt the covers being wrenched out of his hands and he screamed.

'Jake!'

Jake squinted into the bright light. His father stood over him, and it was morning.

'What's the matter, buddy? You were shouting in your sleep.' Dad sat down on the bed and stretched out a hand to brush Jake's sweat-slick hair out of his eyes.

'The seals,' said Jake. He felt confused and thirsty. It should still have been night. He should be soaking wet. He shouldn't be alive. There were no sounds now but the chirrup of a few birds in the trees behind the house.

'Just a bad dream, mate.' Dad patted his leg. 'Do you want a glass of water?'

Jake nodded. He knew it hadn't been a dream — it had been so real. And yet here it was, morning; here was his dad, and the seals — people, creatures, whatever they were — had gone. And he couldn't deny it to himself — the woman who had stolen the skin, who had swum in the water as if she were a part of it, was Cara. He looked with panic at the ground and the sealskin had gone. But when he looked at his closet, he could just make out its dark shape inside. Had he put it away after all, before he went to sleep? His head hurt. Jake gulped the cold water down while Dad stood and watched. He looked thoughtful.

'I feel terrible that I haven't been around for you more. It's this damn book, I'm sorry. It was supposed to be finished before you came, and I have this deadline. I've been so distracted, too. I just can't seem to concentrate.'

Jake shrugged and handed the glass to his father. 'It's fine,' he said, and lay back down. He didn't feel fine.

'No, it's not. Look, I'm not going to do any work today. Let's go for that boat ride I promised you. The weather looks much better today. We'll take the rods and do some fishing. What do you say?'

Jake thought about Cara and the seal-people and hesitated. But he pushed the thought aside — it was only a dream, after all. Everything looked so normal now that it was daytime.

'Just the two of us?' he asked. 'Okay.'

10

As Jake climbed in, the fishing rods clattered in the bottom of the dinghy. The life jacket scratched his chin. He wished they didn't have to wear them, but Dad insisted. His dad pushed the boat out a little way, then jumped in. His jeans were rolled up and beads of salt water clung to the dark hairs on his legs. He grabbed the oars, slotted the rowlocks into their holes and began rowing in earnest.

It was the perfect day for it: blue sky with a few puffs of cloud skating across it, and a light breeze that wasn't too cold. Jake enjoyed the sound of the pull of the oars, and the bucking motion of the little boat. He sat at the front and had to twist his body to see where they were headed: out past the island in Island Bay.

'That should do it,' said Dad, and he swiftly lifted the oars out and lay them on either side of the boat. He stood up, crouching, so the boat didn't shudder from side to side, and pulled the cord on the outboard motor. It spluttered a few times but didn't catch.

'Come on,' said Dad. 'Stupid thing. It's got plenty of petrol in it.'

He pulled the cord so hard Jake thought he was going to topple over with the effort, but at the last second, the engine coughed and roared to life.

'There,' said Dad, but there was no point in saying anything else: the motor was so loud it drowned out everything they could have said to each other. Instead Jake turned his face back towards the open sea and felt the breeze on his face turn to a wind as they picked up speed. He felt like a dog must feel with its head out the window of a moving car — maybe he should let his tongue loll out of his mouth.

Dad found his usual spot, around the other side of the island. His method was to keep going until the island lined up with a house on the hill that had a tower, so the tower looked like a birthday candle on top of the island's cake. He reckoned that was the best spot for snapper. Sometimes there were others out near here, but their boats were usually bigger, with more powerful engines. Today, they were alone. White flecks danced across the wind-chopped water. Luckily, Jake had never had a problem with sea-sickness.

'Do you want me to bait your hook?' Dad asked.

'No, I'll do it.' Jake took the frozen squid bait, chopped a piece off with Dad's big fishing knife, then inched it onto the hook, taking care not to catch his fingers.

'Good job!' Dad said as he deftly baited his own hook and let the line on his fishing rod drop with a fizz.

Jake's sinker made a bloop as it hit the water, and with it the white blob of bait disappeared on its way to the ocean floor. His hands were cold as they gripped the rod, but he felt such exquisite anticipation, it didn't matter. What would find his bait? Would he feel the sudden pull of a kahawai? Or the pecking of a mullet?

They sat without speaking, with the lap of water at the bottom of the dinghy the only sound. Jake closed his eyes and listened to the wind singing in his ears. He wished he'd worn a hat. Suddenly his rod jumped in his hand. He snapped his eyes open. 'A bite!' he said.

'Me too,' said his father, grinning. 'Here we go.'

Jake imagined the school of fish swarming around their lines, diving at the bait.

'I think mine's gone,' said Dad, and started winding in his rod. Jake was about to do the same when he felt another almighty tug, then his rod was dancing in his hands. He gripped it lightly as the end of it bent over almost double. His heart started to beat faster and he let out a small shout. Dad put his own rod down and reached for Jake's.

'No!' Jake cried. 'Let me! I've got it.'

His dad smiled and sat back to watch, poised on his seat to jump in if he was needed.

Jake wound the reel, with some difficulty. Instead of the fast action when the rod was empty, his wrist moved in jerks. And all the time the fish at the other end fought.

'It must be huge!' shouted Jake, excitement making him loud.

'Maybe it's a kingfish,' said Dad. 'Keep going, buddy! You're doing a great job.'

Finally, when Jake thought his aching wrist might fall off, he caught a flash of silver in the dull water. The fish was darting here and there, trying to take the line with it, but Jake had it. He lifted it out of the water and it danced like a whirling dervish on the hook.

'Oh, it's not as big as I thought,' he said. He watched the fish thumping around on the bottom of the boat and let his dad catch it and stand on it while he worked the hook out of its jaws.

'Those kahawai,' said his dad, 'they have a ton of fight in them. They always feel bigger than they are. But look at it, Jake! It's a decent size all right — enough for dinner tonight.'

Jake smiled. 'We'd better catch some more, just in case.'

'That's the spirit.' Dad took the knife and sliced the fish's gullet. Dark blood spurted out and he held the kahawai over the edge of the boat, letting the blood drip into the water. It formed drops on the surface, then blurred and blended with the sea. Jake had forgotten about this part. When he was younger he'd had to look away, but you had to bleed the fish as soon as you caught it or the meat wouldn't taste good.

They re-baited their hooks and dropped their lines. Almost immediately Dad brought up another, and then another, while Jake mostly brought up an empty hook to be baited again. He caught another kahawai, but it was too small so they threw it back. He watched it dance back down through the murk to the bottom. He wondered if it would tell its friends to stop eating the free food — that there were consequences!

'This wind's come up,' said his dad. Jake felt it tossing his hair around, and the boat started rocking. He looked out to where the wind was coming from and saw only a wall of mist, advancing towards them across the sea.

'Dad.' He pointed. His father turned and Jake saw a look of alarm cross his face. Within seconds, the mist was upon them, swirling in the breeze. Waves began to grow beside them. 'Pull in your line,' said Dad. 'Right now.'

Jake silently did as he was told, and placed the rod in the bottom of the boat.

'Grab the anchor.' Dad was on his feet, crouched low, moving towards the outboard motor. Jake struggled with the heavy anchor, but he could tell as he pulled that it had already come loose, that they had already stated drifting. But for how long? And in which direction? He could no longer see the shore, or even the island. He wasn't even sure which way it was. The wind didn't help — each gust seemed to come from a different point. Don't panic, he thought. Dad'll get us out of here.

But his father was having trouble with the outboard motor. It spluttered and coughed again and would only roar to life for a second before dying.

'We're going to have to row for it! Swap places.' He had to shout over the sound of the wind and the sloshing of the waves. Jake moved to the stern while Dad took up his place in the centre of the boat. He carefully lowered the rowlocks in place and began to row. How did he know which way to go?

Dad rowed for what seemed like hours. Jake's stomach grumbled and he pulled out a sandwich from his pocket. He took a bite and suddenly thought, what if they were lost out here for days? He took two small bites and then put the rest back in his pocket. They could always eat raw fish if they were desperate. He was thirsty too, but they had only brought two small water bottles. Best to wait until they were really desperate. He imagined them drifting for days until they were finally rescued by a huge container ship, which would spot them just as it was about to plough over them and continue on its way.

He looked up. His father had stopped rowing. The wind had died down but the mist still surrounded them. It had become still and quiet as quickly as it had become rough. Jake shivered and half expected a ghost pirate ship to cruise silently by, with cutlasses and bare skulls leering at them, but they were all alone.

'I'm not sure which direction we're headed.' Dad hung his head, as if he were ashamed.

'It's okay,' said Jake. 'We've got our life jackets on. And look, the wind has stopped. We'll be fine.' But he didn't feel fine, and he knew his voice betrayed him. It was eerie out there on the water, who knew how far from home? And he had never seen his father look so unsure.

'Hey,' said his dad. He moved down to sit next to Jake. They huddled together. It was like a bad dream. Jake thought about what had happened the night before, at the beach. But that had been a dream, hadn't it? Maybe it *had* happened. He found himself shuddering uncontrollably. Dad pulled him tight.

Then, in the stillness, they heard a splashing sound. Jake turned to look behind them and saw ripples in the water. Big ripples, not like the ones a fish leaves. Could it be . . . were there sharks out here? Things were going from bad to worse. At least the waves had gone, and they were safe in their boat. But what if the shark was big enough to come up underneath them and rip them over?

He looked at the water below, but saw nothing. He closed his eyes. He would prefer not to see it coming, he decided.

'Hello,' said Dad. 'Who have we got here?'

Jake opened his eyes and found himself looking down at a pair of shiny eyes in the water. A small seal floated beside the boat, staring at them. He smiled in relief. Not a shark, then.

The seal kept looking at them.

'We're lost,' Jake said. 'Can you help us get back to shore?'

The seal's nose wrinkled, as though looking at them in disdain. It dived under the boat and disappeared.

'I guess it wasn't in the mood for helping us,' said Dad, chuckling. But then his voice grew grave again. 'We might just have to wait for the mist to clear and find out where we are.' He looked into the sky. 'If we could see the sun we could work out which way was north.' But the sky was a uniform grey, hanging heavily above them. It was so dark it felt as though night could fall at any moment, when in fact it was probably only lunchtime.

They sat waiting for another few minutes. Jake took another bite of his sandwich — he was starving.

The seal popped its head out of the water again. It watched Jake eating.

'Can we give it a fish?' Jake asked.

'Sure.' His dad picked one, the smallest kahawai, from the bucket. He held it out to the seal, who seemed to smile as it took the fish in its jaws. With a toss of the head, the fish disappeared down the seal's gullet in one go. It reminded Jake of something but he couldn't think what. It was nice to see the seal eating, but Jake was still hungry, and he was scared.

'What if we don't make it back to shore?' he asked his dad. 'We'll have to eat fish.' His clothes were damp, and he shivered. A hot tear sprang to his eye and he didn't have time to wipe it away before it fell on his cheek.

'Hey, hey,' said his father. 'We'll be fine. Don't worry.' He looked determined suddenly, and took up the oars again.

As he put them in place, the seal dived under the water again and emerged a few metres away. It turned onto its side and waved a flipper in the air.

Jake wiped his cheek. 'I think it wants us to follow.'

'I doubt that very much,' said Dad, but he rowed a few strokes towards the seal anyway. It dived down again and came up further away. Every time the dinghy got close to it, the seal submerged itself, only to re-emerge a distance away, always looking back at them, sometimes waving a flipper again. They rowed for half an hour. Dad's face was beaded with sweat and his cheeks were red. He was breathing fast.

Jake's heart was beating hard. Could the seal really be showing them the way home? Then he had a terrible thought. Perhaps it knew somehow that he had stolen the sealskin, and it was leading them further and further out to sea as a punishment. But just as he was about to tell his father to stop, to turn around, he gave a shout.

'The island!' Through the mist, the island emerged like a giant crouching turtle. Beyond it, the mist was retreating, the sky was thinning to blue and the curve of Island Bay was coming into view. The seal went under for the last time, and Jake couldn't see where it had come up. But by then, it didn't matter. They knew the way home.

II

A terrible storm developed that afternoon. Jake sat inside with his father watching the sea whip itself into a frenzy. The house shook and moaned.

'I can't believe I took you out there without checking the weather forecast,' said his dad. 'I'm so sorry, Jake. We could have been out there in this. I never would have forgiven myself.'

'It's a good thing that seal showed us the way home.'

'Yes, how extraordinary. I suppose it was just chasing fish, and the fish were moving with the current. The tide was going in, after all. But it seemed like it was waiting for us, didn't it?'

'It was.'

His father ruffled his hair. 'Then if you say that's what happened, that's what happened. It was an adventure anyway.'

Dad lit a fire and they huddled around it. Jake wondered how Ted was getting on in his little cottage. He hoped the sea didn't come right up into the house. What about Jessie? Was she scared? He wished he could get on his bike and go and see her, to tell her about the seal that had saved their lives. She would believe him.

After dinner, they toasted marshmallows on sticks in the glowing embers of the fire, while Dad told him stories. Jake liked to close his eyes and listen to the sound of his father's voice wash over him, taking him to faraway places. He felt truly happy when he was here, sitting next to his father in the warm light. He wished he could live here, go to school in Wellington, but it was complicated, because he also wanted to live with his mother, and it just wasn't possible to have both his parents in the same house. Besides, if Dad had a new girlfriend, there might not be many nights like this left, just the two of them. He had to savour this moment because what if Cara moved in? What if they had a baby? It was bad enough that he had to share his mum with Davey and Greg. He didn't want to have it happen all over again with Dad.

He found his thoughts drifting to what Jessie had said to him about the sealskin, and to the horrible dream he'd had that had felt so real. He was feeling a little scared about going to bed tonight.

'Dad, do you know about selkies?'

'Seal-people? Sure, I know the legend. I think I used to tell you about them when you were small. But I've got news for you, kiddo — they were just fairy stories. If you're hoping to catch a beautiful maiden by hiding its skin, you're out of luck. All those seals at Red Rocks are male anyway. Bachelors who haven't found a mate for the breeding season.'

'That's not what Ted said. He said some were girl seals.'

'Well, I'll believe that when I see it for myself. Why do you ask?'

'Can you tell me again? The story?'

'Aren't you a bit old for fairy tales?'

Jake blushed. 'Okay, forget about it.' He stabbed at a marshmallow with his stick.

'Hey, don't be like that,' said Dad. 'You're very tetchy these days. I'd be happy to tell you what I remember.'

Jake closed his eyes as Dad shifted on his cushion on the floor, leaning his back against the couch.

'The story comes from Celtic and Norse cultures that live by the sea, like the Orkney Islands. It goes that there was once a fisherman who was very lonely. All the women in his village were either very old or they were already married. He longed to have a wife to cook for him and keep him warm at night, and to give him children to fill his tiny cottage with laughter. Yes, I know, it's not a very modern fairy story — don't let your mum catch you talking about women like that.

'Anyway, one day he got back from a fishing trip and he met a woman on the shore who looked a little lost and who was clad only in seaweed. He took her home and gave her clothes to wear and food to eat. She was very quiet and very, very beautiful and he fell deeply in love with her. He asked her to marry him but she said that she couldn't, that she was a selkie and she must return to her people. But he locked her in a room and went out looking for her skin. He found it hidden in a cave in the rocks and took it home and put it in a chest in the cellar, which he locked tightly.

'The woman could not return to her people

without her skin. She searched and searched in vain. When she came back from looking for it, she agreed to marry him and live with him until she could find it. She learned to cook and she kept him warm at night, but every day when he went out fishing, she roamed the coast, always hunting for her skin, unaware that it was right underneath her, in the cellar.

'The fisherman was very much in love with her, but she refused to give him children because she said it would be unfair on them when she returned to the sea. As the years went by and she did not find her skin, she grew sadder and sadder. She hardly ate anything and she wasn't much more than skin and bones. Soon she was so weak she couldn't get out of bed. The fisherman sent for the doctor, who told him the terrible news that he didn't expect her to live much longer. The fisherman was devastated. He spent the whole night crying, and in the morning he knew what he had to do. He loved her very much and didn't want to lose her, but if he gave her back her skin, she would finally be happy and free and she would live.

'The woman could barely open her eyes when the sun came through the curtains, but there on her bed was her skin. Summoning the last of her energy, she took it and left the house, walking down to the sea without so much as a goodbye to the man who had loved her but who had held her prisoner for so long. Once she was wearing her skin, he never saw her again.

'I think that's how it goes,' said Dad.

'But why would a selkie come on land if she risked getting stuck as a human?' asked Jake. 'Why was she there in the first place?'

'I don't know the answer to that. But if you had the chance to transform yourself into another sort of creature, wouldn't you? Just to see what it was like?'

Jake smiled. 'Yeah. I'd love to be a bird. Or a dolphin!'

'Well, there you go. Maybe a seal, even.'

Jake remembered the dream he'd had, the

feeling of freedom as he'd spun through the water. And then the terror, when the skin had been taken from him and he'd started to drown. 'Not a seal,' he said.

'Sorry I'm not a better storyteller,' said Dad. 'That's my version of the myth anyway. I'm sure you could find a book about it if you wanted.'

'Maybe I will,' said Jake. He shrugged. 'It doesn't matter though. I was just curious. Jessie thinks selkies are real.'

'Well, she's younger than you, Jake. Little kids believe things. You did. Don't be mean to her about it. I think it's nice when you can believe in things like that for so long.' He ruffled Jake's hair. 'Okay, mister?'

Jake smiled. 'Sure. Maybe I believe in them too. Just a little bit.'

It was Dad's turn to smile. 'And that is nothing to be ashamed of. We could all use a little bit of magic in our lives, don't you think?'

They sat there for a while longer. Jake watched his father's face while he stared into the fire, looking as though his mind had wandered elsewhere. He hadn't shaved for a few days and his beard had come in thick and fast. Jake was shocked to see how much grey was in it. He turned to the fire and began to make out shapes in the flames that curved and flickered around the logs. Faces, seals . . .

'Bedtime for you, mister. Come on, look at you, you're nodding off.'

Jake allowed himself to be led into his room. He was so tired he just flopped onto the bed. He was already wearing his pyjamas, so Dad just stuffed him under the covers. The sheets felt alarmingly cold for a bit, but they soon warmed with the heat from his body and before he knew it, he was asleep, with the sound of the rain pelting the roof and the wind scrabbling at the windows.

He was awoken some hours later by a booming sound. He sat up, alarmed, and his room was suddenly lit up as bright as day before being plunged into darkness again. A few seconds later another crash, like two planes colliding directly overhead. He lay back down again — just thunder and lightning, but boy did it feel close. He wondered if he was safe in his bed, whether lightning could find you, even inside a house. He waited with anticipation for the next flash — the storm was so close now. There it was, lighting up the clothes strewn around the room, the open closet, inside which the sealskin lay. Jake jumped as the thunder struck almost immediately. It was right above him! And — what was that smell? Hot and meaty, but mixed with mud and salt. He was blinded by the previous flash and he looked in the darkness towards the wardrobe. Surely the smell wasn't coming from there? He jumped out of bed to slam the wardrobe door shut and as the door connected there was a startling flash of white and an almighty BOOM! Jake was only a metre from the curtainless window and in the puff of light he saw a face! It flickered in the light, looking in at him, a pale face with huge dark eyes and a wild crown of red hair that was being whipped around in the wind and the rain.

Jake screamed, but another flash drowned him out. Cara appeared to look straight at him. The next second the world was dark again and Jake waited, holding his breath for more lightning and thunder, but it didn't come. When finally a gentle flicker ignited, the woman was gone and the storm was moving away with her. The roll of thunder was a long time afterwards and it sounded like a distant cannon.

Jake got back into bed and pulled the covers up to his ears, but he was too shaken and scared to go to sleep. He got out of bed again and padded through the house to his father's room. He got in bed beside him and Dad moved over to let him in.

'Scared of the storm?' His father's voice was thick with sleep.

'Yeah,' said Jake, and he almost felt safe again, with his father sleeping beside him. But still he could not sleep. He listened to the storm moving further and further away, and every night noise sounded like someone trying to get into the house. And now there was one thing he knew for sure. He knew what it was that Cara was looking for. She had come for her skin. Was this why she had befriended his father? Had she sensed her skin was near? And was it possible his father was falling in love with her? He knew now what he had to do.

12

As soon as it started to get light outside, Jake got out of bed while his father snored. He hardly ever got up before his dad. The storm had completely gone and the sky outside was streaked with pink and gold. Jake moved quietly into his room. He took his backpack and opened the wardrobe, expecting to be hit by the horrible odour again, but only when he brought the sealskin right up to his face did he smell it.

It was milder than the night before, but had the same musky, dirty essence.

He stuffed it into his bag, but it was too big and stuck out the top. He went into the kitchen and got a rubbish bag from the drawer, which he used to cover it, to protect it from the weather, but also to hide it. His hands shook as he pulled the plastic over the backpack. What if he couldn't get there in time? What if Cara was outside waiting for him?

'What are you up to?'

Jake spun around to see his father standing in the doorway, rubbing his eyes and yawning. 'You're up early. Do you want some breakfast?'

'I had some already,' lied Jake. 'It's a nice day. Can I go and see Jessie?'

'If you want.' Dad walked to Jake's window and looked out. 'It's so calm out there now. You'd never know there'd been a storm.' He turned. 'Wrap up warm, though. It's cold at this time of the morning. I should know.'

Jake nodded and grabbed his coat. He tried

not to look at his bag in the corner of the room, in case Dad saw what he was looking at and asked questions. He waited for his father to leave the room, but he just stood there, yawning and scratching his thickening beard.

'Well,' said Dad. 'I'm off for a shower. Can't seem to wake up this morning. I've got a lot of work on today, since yesterday was a write-off. You okay with that?'

'Yes, fine.' Jake started tapping his toes and willing his father to go, which he did. As soon as Jake heard the shower start up, he picked up the bag and threw it on his back, making for the front door.

'What's in the bag?'

Jake spun around. His dad was advancing down the hall towards him, a towel wrapped around his waist.

'Nothing,' said Jake. 'Just a jacket. And my lunch.'

'But you're wearing your jacket. What are you up to? I thought you were behaving strangely.'

Jake didn't know what to say. He turned away, his heart beating faster. Dad stopped a metre away, scrutinising him. 'Jake . . .' There was a stern warning in his voice.

Jake opened the front door, but to his surprise and horror, his dad lunged forward and grabbed the bag, wrestling it off Jake's back.

'Hey!' said Jake as he lost his balance and fell onto his backside. He struggled to his feet, disoriented by the scuffle, but his father was intent on the bag and unapologetic.

Dad held the bag up to his face and sniffed. 'It pongs. What is it?' He started to pull the plastic bag off the backpack and Jake tried unsuccessfully to stop him. His father was just too strong and batted him away as if he were an annoying insect. In the struggle, Jake came away with nothing but empty plastic wafting in his face.

Dad just stood there, staring at the open bag with the sealskin sticking out the top of it. The shower was still running down the hall, and steam started to roll out of the bathroom like mist.

Jake looked at the sealskin, aghast. Dad's face betrayed his racing mind; it showed confusion, worry. Jake tried to push away the guilt he was feeling. After all, he had found it, not stolen it; he had nothing to hide, or to be ashamed of. Dad looked up at him and seemed to snap out of a trance. He pointed at Jake, as if telling him not to move a muscle, and backed silently down the hallway to the bathroom, disappearing inside with the bag. Jake heard the shower being shut off and the rattle of the latch as the window opened. Cold air rushed into the house, dispelling the steam and coming for Jake like a wraith. He shivered.

Dad emerged still clutching the sealskin and still wearing nothing but a towel. He stared at the skin in amazement, then rubbed his cheek against it. He buried his face in and drew a big breath. It would have made Jake gag, he was sure of it, but Dad's face came away sweetened, as though he had been smelling roses.

He grabbed Jake's arm and pulled him into the living room.

'Sit down,' he said. 'Wait here.'

Jake sat on an armchair while Dad put the sealskin down carefully on the couch and left the room. Jake stared at the skin, and thought about jumping up and grabbing it, running out of the house with it. But what sort of trouble would he get in if he did that? Was it worse to leave Cara without her skin or to disobey his father? The more he thought about it, and the longer his father took to come back, the more he realised which was worse. He made up his mind and was preparing to lunge for it when his father came back into the room, dressed. Jake was disturbed by the fact that he hadn't said anything about it yet. Did he even know what it was?

'So.' Dad sat down on the couch and put one protective hand over the skin. 'Tell me. Where did you get it?'

Jake looked at the floor. 'I found it. In a cave at Red Rocks.'

'And you know what this is?'

'Of course I do. It's a sealskin.'

'How long have you had it?'

'Ages. Since my first day at the beach.'

'Oh, Jake.' His dad gave a big sigh. 'Why have you had it all this time and not told me?'

Jake looked up at him, into his eyes. His father had a wild look to him, with his fresh beard and wiry, sticking-out hair. 'Because it was mine. I found it. Besides, I knew you'd want to take it off me. Give it away to a museum or something. I just wanted to keep it for a while.'

He couldn't tell him the truth. That the skin had spoken to him somehow, that it had made him possessive, that it felt like a dark secret that only he should know about. That he had finally worked out what Cara was looking for. And that he had to give it back to her so that she could return to the sea and leave them alone.

They sat there in silence as, outside, Jake heard the world waking up. A few cars hummed past; a pair of birds fought outside the window.

Jake waited for his dad to speak.

'And where were you going with it, Jake?'

'I was putting it back where I found it. So whoever it belongs to can have it back.'

'Whoever it belongs to,' his father echoed, his voice flat. 'Do you know who that might be?'

Jake said nothing, but his cheeks started to get hot. How much did his dad know? Only one way to find out. 'Do you?'

Dad stared at him. His face was like a statue's, immobile stone. Finally, he said quietly, 'I have an idea.'

Jake felt like crying. What had he done? If only he'd left the stupid sealskin where it was. Now that it was out of his hands, he began to feel its power over him draining away. He wanted to get it away from Dad, not so he could have it for himself, but so he could get rid of it.

'Is this why you were asking me about the selkies?' asked his dad.

Jake couldn't lie. It was too obvious; would have been too much of a coincidence.

'Yes,' he said. 'Jessie thought it might belong to someone.'

'Someone who would have to stay in human form if they couldn't find it. If it was . . .' His voice trailed away as he turned his head to gaze out the window. 'If it was hidden from them.'

The words Jake wanted to say caught in his throat. He tried to clear it.

Dad stood up, still looking out the window. He'd be able to see the sea from where he was. He was deep in thought. He tucked the sealskin under his arm.

'I'm going to hold on to this for a while.'

'Dad, please, let me have it back. Let me put it back.'

'No.'

'Please.'

'I said no!' his father roared at him suddenly, making Jake jump in his chair and a cold sweat spring to his forehead. He'd never heard his dad's voice so deep, like an animal growl, and for the first time that he could remember, in his whole life, he felt afraid of him. And yet, there was something about his father's manner that was familiar. It was how he himself had behaved when Jessie had tried to take the skin from him.

Jake backed from the room, afraid to take his eyes off his father. 'Can I go now?' he asked.

'Yes,' said Dad, his voice calm again, but flat, like a robot. 'Yes, that's a good idea. You go and play with Jessie. Come back later. In time for dinner.'

Jake wrenched open the front door and fled, slamming it behind him. His bike was around the side of the house, where it had been sheltered from the worst of the storm, but the seat and handlebars were slick and when he sat on it, he felt the water seep into the seat of his pants.

He pedalled as hard as he could. Every now and then a car coasted by him on the quiet road. The sea was like a polished stone, the waves nothing more than a gentle rise and fall of water. The sound of his breathing filled his ears, keeping time with the swish of his tyres on the gravelly road.

Once he hit the beach road, his legs began to tire and he was hot, but he pushed on. He passed the small, sad mound of a dead little blue penguin by the side of the road. Normally he would have gotten off his bike to look at it, but this time he didn't stop. The beach was littered with broken logs and seaweed, thrown up by the storm. He put his head down, and pedalled on. His lungs were burning and his legs were beginning to feel numb by the time he came to Ted's cabin. Smoke was coming from the chimney, and it was safe; it hadn't been swept away in the night as he had feared.

He dumped his bike with a clatter on the path outside the hut and took off his jacket. Then he knocked on the door.

Ted answered. 'Jake.' He looked surprised to see him. 'Thought we'd seen the last of you. Jessie said you'd had a fight, ya silly kids.'

Jake's stomach flipped. 'Did she say what about?'

'Nope.' He shook his head. 'She really didn't

want to tell me, so I left her to her sulk. Haven't seen her.'

Jake tried to peer into the cottage. 'But didn't she stay here last night?'

Ted looked caught out. 'Oh. Yes. Yes, of course. She just got up before I did. Must have slipped out for a walk.'

Jake jiggled on his toes. 'I really need to talk to her.'

Ted looked at him for a few seconds, as if making up his mind about something.

'All right,' he said. 'Come in. I'll go and find her.'

'I can go — where would she be? At the rocks?'

Ted shot out a hand and grabbed his arm. 'No, boy. Really. You wait here.'

Jake couldn't argue with the tone of the old man's voice. He went inside and sat down. Ted made for the door, then hesitated. He crossed back and grabbed some clothes that were drying by the fire, including a black jersey. Then he was gone, the door banging behind him.

13

Jake went to the window and watched Ted's back disappearing in the direction of Red Rocks. He scanned the beach, scared that he would see Cara — what would he say to her if he did? Would he tell her about the skin? Perhaps he shouldn't have come looking for Jessie and should have looked for Cara instead. But he was here now — he'd wait and see what Jessie had to say. He got himself a drink of water and as he stood drinking it, looked around the room. A glint of gold, behind a pile of newspapers on a shelf, caught his eye. He put the water glass down and went to investigate. It was a photo frame, carefully polished, which seemed strange in the shabby house. In the photograph, a man sat with a little girl on his knee. Beside him was another girl, a few years older, and in the back, a woman. The woman looked a little like Cara, and the older girl a little like Jessie — they had the same pointy faces and dark eyes — but it definitely wasn't them, and besides, the photograph was black and white so he couldn't tell what colour their hair was. The man was handsome, with dark hair and a beard. Ted, when he was younger, surely. Something nagged at Jake about the photo, but he couldn't place it, so he put it back carefully where he had found it, and sat down to wait.

Soon the door opened and Ted came in with Jessie. She wore holey shorts and the black jumper Ted had taken from by the fire. She didn't smile when she saw Jake, but turned to the old man and said, 'You can go now,' as if he was her servant and she was dismissing him. Jake waited for Ted to tell her off, as his dad would if he spoke to him like that; instead, Ted shrugged, murmured something about going fishing, and left them alone.

'It is about the skin, is it not?'

Jake nodded. He knitted his hands together, staring at his entwined fingers.

'It's Cara's, isn't it?' he said. 'You told her I had it. She's hanging around us to get it back.'

'No. I did not tell her, Jake. If I had she might have . . .' Her voice trailed away and she looked pained. 'Jake, she would have hurt you. I could not tell her. I am scared of her, of what she could do.'

'Then why was she at my window last night?'

'She has been looking everywhere for it. You have seen her, just walking the streets, the beach, have you not?'

Jake nodded.

'She has sensed it is near but she does not know for sure. Ted has explained it to me. He says that if a skin is taken, the selkie will be drawn to the person who has it, but may not realise why.'

'So she was drawn to me?'

'Yes, but you are so young. She might think it is your father that is drawing her to your house. She might think she is in love with him. If you put it back where you found it, she will go. If you keep it, Jake, you are in danger. She must not find out that you have it. And she must be able to return to the water, to be with her people, or she will die.'

Jake sat down and covered his face with his hands. 'I tried to bring it back. But Dad found it. I think he's in love with her or something. He wouldn't let me have it.'

Jessie went pale. 'Does he know what she is?'

'I don't think he did before, but he said he's lonely. He knows about selkies; he just didn't believe in them. But I think now he does. I think he's going to keep it and not let her go.'

Jessie shook her head sadly. 'I did not know your father was lonely. I thought he was safe. It is always the lonely men who are the most dangerous. That's what Ted says.'

'How does he know so much?'

'He just does.' She did not invite further questions. Jake studied her face. She seemed to have grown up so much in the time they had known each other. She wasn't like a little kid. Sometimes the way she talked was like a wise old woman.

'You have to steal it back, Jake, and you have to do it soon.'

Jake was scared to go home. Dad had told him to be home in time for dinner but it was only lunchtime. Still, he had to make a start at looking for the skin. He had left the house without eating anything and he was starving. Jessie stayed at the shack and Jake biked slowly towards home. The wind had started to come up again, and grey clouds were advancing from the ocean like a thick blanket. The beach road was dotted with people out walking, attracted by the sunny morning. Some of them were now looking at the sky, frowning, wondering whether to turn back.

The car park at the beginning of the beach road was fuller than he had seen before. Dark figures stood in the unmanned information centre, looking at maps and reading about the seals and about the rocks, which were burnished red by iron oxide. Or, according to Maori legend, by the spilled blood of the explorer Kupe and his daughters. What the information didn't say, thought Jake, was that if you find a sealskin in a cave, leave it there and run for your life!

He left the car park and crossed the road, his tyres humming. As he came around a corner, he saw two familiar figures standing with their backs to a brick wall, smoking cigarettes. It was the two boys, Mark and his blonde friend, who had been torturing the friendly dog. Just as Jake thought about moving to the other side of the road to avoid them, Mark stepped in front of him. Jake braked and tried to swerve, but Mark grabbed the handlebars as he went past and Jake's wheels skidded out from under him, knocking him sideways. The gravel road rose up to meet his hands and he felt a sharp pain through his wrist. He rolled to one side to avoid any cars that might come around the corner, and sat up.

'Nice bike,' sneered Mark. He had a fresh cut on his lip, as if he'd been fighting. 'What d'ya reckon, Dan? Too good for this dickhead.' He was still holding the bike, and his friend came to join him.

'I reckon,' said Dan. He had a sullen face, with small blue eyes and blonde eyelashes, which should have given him an angelic appearance, but somehow had the opposite effect.

Jake's face burned and he cradled his sore wrist. Hot tears welled in his eyes. He was furious with himself: he didn't want to give these boys the satisfaction of making him cry. But the pain was real and he couldn't help it.

'Please give it back,' he said. 'My wrist really hurts.'

Dan and Mark looked at each other and laughed. 'So polite!' said Dan, then his voice kicked into a high and whingey register. '*Please give it back*,' he mimicked. '*My wrist really hurts. Boo hoo hoo.*' He rubbed his eyes, pretending to cry. 'What a baby.'

'Come on,' said Mark, straddling the bike. Dan jumped on the carrier at the rear, and the two boys wobbled off on it, back in the direction of the beach, cackling.

'Hey!' called Jake. But the boys made a rude gesture without turning back and disappeared around the corner, leaving Jake there on the ground, rubbing his wrist, with furious tears in his eyes.

14

It wasn't just the pain, or the bullies, that were bringing the tears. Once he started, he couldn't stop thinking about what a mess he'd gotten himself, and his dad, into. It was all his fault.

He sat there on the curb for a long time. A few cars went past and the occupants gave him curious looks, but nobody stopped, and the boys didn't come back. Eventually he stood up and walked towards home, passing the house with the dog. The Labrador was lying at the front doorstep and as Jake went by their eyes met. This time, it didn't wag its tail, just raised its head and watched him go by.

'I'm sorry,' Jake whispered, but the dog just sighed and laid its head back on its paws. Jake wished he could make the dog understand him.

The front door was locked when he finally got home. He found the key in its hiding place under a loose brick in the wall and let himself in. The house was quiet but Jake knew instantly that Cara had been there. The rooms smelt of the sea. All except Jake's room, and he breathed a sigh of relief that she hadn't been in there. Although, why would she? The skin was no longer there.

He sat down on his bed, feeling sorry for himself. Where was his dad? How could he just go out and leave him like this? He really needed to talk to him, to tell him about the bike, and what the boys had done. Dad would probably call the police. Jake would feel safer once it was out of his hands. He crossed the room to the window and looked out. What if the boys knew where he lived? He really didn't want to face them again.

Then it came to him. If Dad was out, and Cara had been here, his father must have hidden the sealskin somewhere. Now was his chance to find it! But where to start?

Ignoring his rumbling stomach, he went into his dad's bedroom. The curtains were shut and he disturbed a blowfly, which buzzed lazily from the lightshade to the wall, where it sat watching him. Jake knelt on the floor and looked under the bed. He pulled out a cardboard box, which brought dust bunnies with it, tickling his nose and making him sneeze. But all that the box had inside was a pile of papers — research notes for Dad's book probably. Jake shuffled through them quickly and something caught his eye. He pulled out a photograph of himself and his dad taken a couple of summers ago. Jake was smiling into the camera, hair bleached by the sun and his freckly nose pink with sunburn. Dad had his arm around Jake's shoulder and Jake was shocked to see how sad his father looked, as though he might be about to cry. It was not long after his parents had broken up.

He looks lonely, thought Jake, and dropped the photo back in the box, brushing the thought away. He didn't have time to be looking through these things. Dad could be back any moment, and worse — Cara could be with him. He had to find the skin before they got back.

He pushed the box back under the bed, wincing as the pain in his wrist flared again, and stood up. Next, he tried the closet. More boxes, which, once he had struggled to lift and open them with his one good arm, turned out to contain more papers. He sat down on the bed. This wasn't going to be as easy as he'd thought. But of course — why would his dad hide the skin so close? It would have to be somewhere

Cara couldn't find if she went looking.

He thought about the selkie story Dad had told him by the fire that night. What had he said about the fisherman? That he had hidden the skin in a chest in the cellar, under the house, and the wife had never known it was right beneath her the whole time.

Jake opened the front door and walked around the small house, looking for a door to the cellar. It didn't take him long to work out that the cottage didn't even have a cellar. It was sitting close to the ground on concrete foundations and there was nothing but a narrow space of dirt under the house.

He looked up at the writing shed. Surely it must be there? He ran up the narrow track and tried the door. Locked of course. He looked in the window and thought about smashing it to try and get in, but then if it wasn't there, his dad would figure out what he was up to and it could spoil his plans to find the skin. He'd just have to take his time. He could see his dad's computer sitting on the desk, untidy stacks of paper teetering beside it. Dad said his deadline had come and gone, so he should be working night and day on his book, and yet, here it was, sitting alone while its author was out. How could Dad earn any money if he didn't finish his book? Jake felt the stab of guilt again — it was his fault that Cara had entered their lives.

Jake searched the rest of the house. He munched on an apple as he looked through the kitchen cupboards, then moved on to the cupboard in the hallway, under the couch, and finally, up the chimney. His hands came away blackened, and when he went to wash them in the bathroom he caught sight of himself in the mirror. Soot marked his face and his eyes were red from crying. The bare bulb hung above his head, casting sharp shadows. He looked like a ghost.

He had just finished washing and drying his face when he heard the front door open and footsteps in the hall.

'He's not home,' he heard his father say. 'His bike's not here.'

A soft, tinkling laugh, and Jake felt ice in his veins. He shivered. His hands were frozen to the basin and as he stared at his face in the mirror he saw it go pale. What should he do? Pretend he wasn't there, and see what they did, what they talked about? Or tell them he was home?

The voices moved into the living room and through to the kitchen, where he could barely hear them. He breathed steadily but quickly, paralysed by indecision. He really didn't want to see Cara. After all, she'd had some kind of spell over him before — what if she still did? Should he go out there and tell her that Dad had the skin, just to get rid of her? But no. Jessie had warned him that she could get angry. He had seen what Jessie could do when she was angry, and he imagined Cara would be much stronger. Then a chilling thought hit him — he had just compared Jessie to Cara, as though

Jessie were a younger, smaller version of her aunt. Could this mean . . . ?

He pushed the thought away. He refused to believe that Jessie was anything other than a normal little girl. But when he closed his eyes to gather himself, he saw Jessie's dark eyes and sharp little teeth, her strange immunity to the cold, the way she didn't seem to mind being wet. Her borrowed clothes. So many things were adding up now in his head that he wanted to yell to shut them out. But he didn't want his dad to know that he was home. Instead, he decided to sneak out, to get away from Cara.

Music had started up in the kitchen. Jake had never heard his dad listen to modern music — just the drone of the radio: the talking kind, or boring classical music. He risked a peek around the door of the living room and through to the kitchen. He could see movement in there, and hear laughter, from both of them.

'How long can you stay?' His father's voice was raised over the music.

'I don't know,' said Cara.

'Forever, I hope!' said Dad with a soppy tone, and Jake winced.

'Maybe,' she said, but quietly, and Jake could have been mistaken.

Suddenly they burst through into the lounge, dancing. Cara was in Dad's arms at first, then she was being spun around, twirling like a ballet dancer, with the skirt of her flower-print dress ballooning around her. Dad's eyes were fixed on her, and one thought flashed into Jake's head: *I've never seen him look so happy.* He was so astonished he forgot that he was supposed to be hiding. As the couple danced, Jake took in the rest of the room. Spread all over the couch were shopping bags, some with food spilling out — wine, chocolate, springy tufts of celery and a stick of French bread — and others with the names of fashion stores emblazoned in gold letters on the side. He looked again at Cara and realised that if he had passed her on the street he might not have recognised her.

Her dirty coat was gone, and over her flowery dress she wore a bright red cardigan. Her feet, for the first time since Jake had known her, had shoes on them, which were silver. Her hair, instead of sticking out wildly around her face, was pulled back into a ponytail, making her appear smaller, more . . . human.

Jake felt sick. They looked so perfect, alone together. Why would his dad want him around any more while Cara was there? He would only get in the way. He stepped back into the hall without being seen. Every muscle in his body felt rigid. He wanted to punch the wall. He went right up to it, fists ready.

Then he stopped. He realised that he could get angry, could run away even, but that he had got himself into this mess and it was up to him to do something about it. Clearly she had Dad under some kind of spell. What else would explain the shopping bags, the expensive-looking shoes on her feet? Dad didn't have any money. It was a struggle for him just to afford Jake's airfare down from Auckland; Jake's mother had paid for half of it. And yet here he was, buying Cara fancy new clothes and expensive food. Jake had to do something.

He turned away from the wall, and gasped. Cara was standing in the hallway, looking at him calmly. She was fixing him with those dark eyes, and Jake felt himself falling into them. He looked away quickly, before she caught him up in her magic.

'Hello, Jake.' Her voice was low and quiet, like distant waves. She came towards him and reached out. Her hand alighted on his bare arm. Her skin was cool and slightly damp and he looked down, alarmed to see thick blue webbing between her fingers.

'Is that Jake?' His father's voice came from the living room, and Cara dropped Jake's arm and stepped away from him. Dad's head popped around the door. 'You're home early.' He didn't look too happy about it. 'We were just going to start cooking some dinner. Why don't you go to the movies? I think one's due to start soon — that one you wanted to see.'

'No thanks,' said Jake.

Dad came towards him, rifling through his pocket. 'Not really a request, mate,' he said. He pulled out a twenty-dollar note and handed it over. 'Off you go. You can bike down. I'll pick you up after since it'll be dark by then.'

Jake took the money and pushed past them, head down. He didn't really want to hang around them anyway, watching them be all lovey-dovey. But once he was outside he remembered that his bike had been stolen. He didn't want to tell his dad in case he got mad — who knew how he would react? His father just wasn't himself at the moment, and Jake didn't want to risk provoking him, so he set off to Island Bay on foot in the dying afternoon light.

15

Of course he was late to the movie, so he sat in the blackness, not following the story and unable to concentrate on it anyway. Giant robots screeched and crunched their way across the screen but he couldn't work out if they were meant to be good or evil. Maybe they were neither — or both. His arm was still throbbing and he couldn't stop his mind from wandering back over the day's awful events: the scrape of his hand on the gravel and the sting of his bike being stolen; his fruitless search through the dusty house; the look on his dad's face when he was with Cara.

It was dark when he came out. The days were still so short at this time of year. His stomach growled despite the packet of nuts he'd eaten. There was no sign of Dad's car, so he stood near the road and waited. Moviegoers, heading in for the next session, stepped around him.

'You okay?' asked one woman.

'Fine, thanks,' he said. 'Just waiting for my dad.'

The woman looked concerned, but said nothing more and disappeared into the cinema. The crowd thinned and evaporated, and Jake was left standing alone, still waiting. He was cold and shoved his hands deep into his pockets.

Finally, one of the theatre staff, a tall young guy with dreadlocks, came out to where he stood.

'Do you need to call someone?' he asked.

His face was kind but Jake couldn't remember his dad's number, so he shook his head and thanked him.

'I'm sure he'll be here soon.' Jake's voice sounded much brighter than he felt. On the inside he was worried Dad had forgotten him altogether. He kicked a nearby lamppost. It was bad enough that his father didn't want to live in the same city as him, even though Jake had practically begged him to come to Auckland when he was younger. But at least Dad usually *tried* to make Jake feel special when he was visiting, despite often being so busy writing. Now he couldn't even remember to pick his own son up from the movies. Jake was just contemplating stomping home in the dark, which he didn't relish, when Dad's dented old car pulled up. Dad beeped the horn, even though Jake had seen him and was already moving towards the curb.

'Sorry, sorry,' said Dad. His voice was vigorous but he didn't really sound remorseful. 'Lost track of time. Hope you didn't have to wait too long.'

Jake said nothing and scrunched angrily down in his seat as they drove away.

'Hey,' said Dad. 'Where's your bike?' He stopped the car. 'We can't leave it there overnight.' He was just about to pull a U-turn, and Jake realised he'd have to tell him.

'No, stop.' He put his hand on Dad's arm. 'I haven't got it. Some kids nicked it.'

'What? Why didn't you say so?' He switched the engine off and turned to look at Jake. 'What happened?'

Jake gave him the censored version of the day, the version he had gone over in his head at the movies. He told him about the boys but not about his conversation with Jessie or the hunt for the sealskin. 'And I hurt my arm.' He held it out. His wrist was nicely bruised now and a warm feeling spread through him when he saw how worried his dad looked as he took it gently in his hands.

'Right,' said Dad. 'I'm calling the police when we get home. Those little gangsters aren't getting away with this. Mate, why didn't you tell me before?'

Jake realised that the story had given Dad a shock — the aura of enchantment around him had slipped and Jake had been able to wriggle his way back in. Now was his chance.

'Because Cara's got you all . . . weird!' he blurted. 'I thought you'd be mad. Or you wouldn't care.' He didn't know which was worse.

'Hey!' said Dad. 'What do you mean?'

'Is she your girlfriend or something now? You bought her all that stuff. You can't afford it. Mum told me you don't have any money.'

Dad paused, weighing up his words carefully. 'Cara's special, Jake. She needs looking after. She doesn't have any money or anywhere to live. We have to be kind to her. She doesn't deserve to be homeless. Nobody does.'

'So, what, is she moving in with you?'

Dad sighed. 'I don't expect you to understand. It's grown-up stuff.'

'But I do understand. It's just what happened with Mum. Greg moved in, and now there's a baby.'

Dad laughed but he didn't look amused. 'Let's not get too far ahead of ourselves, eh?'

'Do you love her?'

'What kind of a question is that?'

'*Do you love her?*'

Dad ran a hand through his thick hair and looked at Jake with serious eyes. 'Yes, Jake, I love her.'

'I knew it.' The magic had enveloped his father. There was no way he could love someone like that after just meeting her. Jake had to do something. He took a deep breath.

'I know what she is, Dad. I know you took her skin and hid it so she'd stay with you.'

Dad put his hands on the steering wheel and stared at them. 'Do you now?'

'You have to give the skin back, or . . .'

'Or what, Jake? Or she'll stay with me?

I'll be happy? Is that so bad?'

'You said yourself, in the story you told me. She won't rest until she's found it. She'll just wander around all the time, looking for it.' Jake dropped his voice to a whisper. 'And then she'll die.'

'Oh, rubbish,' said Dad, swatting the air between them. 'I know what this is, Jake. You're jealous. And I can understand that, with everything that's happened with your mum. But this is what I want.'

'I am *not* jealous,' said Jake, but he was lying.

'Besides,' said Dad. 'She loves me too. It wouldn't make a blind bit of difference if I gave her the skin. Which, I might add, is just a fairy story — you said so yourself. She'd stay with me anyway.'

'Well, prove it, then!' said Jake. 'Give it back and see what happens.'

'Maybe I will.' Dad started up the car again and shifted it roughly into gear. They drove home in an angry silence.

*

Jake woke with a start the next morning, realising he'd lost track of the days. It was Saturday. That meant he was leaving tomorrow, flying back up to Auckland. He only had today to make things right! Cara hadn't been there when they got home from the movies, and Jake and his dad didn't mention her again. Dad had called the police, as he said he would, but they had said there wasn't much they could do, and that Jake and his dad should keep an eye out in case the bike showed up somewhere. Jake had eaten his dinner, then gone to bed. Later, he'd heard the front door click open and light footsteps going past his room.

Sure enough, when he got up, Cara was sitting at the table with Dad, their heads together as they drank tea. Jake slipped past them into the kitchen without saying anything, and stood at the bench while he waited for his toast to cook. Dad came up behind him and pressed the button to re-boil the kettle.

'You off out today?' he asked. He sounded hopeful.

Jake's stomach dropped. His last day before heading back to Mum, Greg and the baby, and his dad was trying to get rid of him. Things were bad. 'Yeah,' said Jake. Then, whispering: 'So have you given it back to her?'

'Shh!' said Dad, and grabbed Jake's sore wrist, roughly.

'Ow!' Jake knew the sound of the kettle coming to the boil would drown out his voice, so he said boldly: 'Where is it, Dad?'

But his dad just frowned and shook his head, and Jake realised then that he would never tell, because deep down his father knew that Cara would leave him as soon as it was in her strange webbed hands.

16

Even without his bike, it didn't take a long time to get out to Ted's cottage to find Jessie. The knot in Jake's stomach made him walk fast, jog even, and his sense of urgency increased as the sun climbed higher in the sky. Tomorrow he would be back on a plane, and who knew what would happen once he was gone? His only hope was getting Jessie to help him.

She came running to meet him when the shack came into sight.

'I knew you would come,' she said. 'You did not find it, did you? I saw Cara last night.'

'Did you say something to her?'

'No, of course not! I said I would not.'

'What did she say?'

'She said that she had not found the skin and that she was preparing to make a life in human form, at least for the time being. That she had found someone to take care of her better than Ted can.'

Jake sat down on the ground. He knew it. He drew his knees up and put his head in his arms.

'What am I going to do?'

He felt a cool hand on his shoulder. Jessie was trying to comfort him.

'We must find it today. We will ask Ted to help.'

Ted sat by the fire, drinking a mug of tea and doing a crossword puzzle in a book. He put it to one side when he saw the look on Jake's face. Jake wondered how much Ted knew about what had been going on.

It was as if Ted had read his mind. He stood up, nodding. 'Ah, young fella. You've got that look about you. It's Cara, isn't it? She's got a hold of your dad.'

Jake bit back tears and nodded.

'He found the skin? At the rocks?'

Jake blushed. 'No, it was me. I hid it. I didn't know she was a selkie. Not until Jessie told me, but even then I didn't believe her.' He felt ashamed of himself. 'Then when I tried to bring it back, Dad stopped me. And by then he'd fallen in love with Cara and it was too late. He's got it. He's hidden it somewhere.' He heard the misery in his own voice.

'This is all my fault,' said Ted.

'Why is it *your* fault?'

'I had no idea that you had the skin, boy. It's my job to keep them safe. If I'd known I would've warned you, so I would. And I wouldn't have let Cara meet your dad. No, you should have told me. At least, Jessie should have told me when she knew.'

Jessie looked at her feet, but said nothing.

Jake spread his hands in front of him. 'What can we do? I can't find the skin. Jessie says we can't tell her he has it.'

'No,' said Ted quickly, 'you mustn't do that. Look, sit down, boy. I've got something you should hear.'

'But I don't have time! We have to find the skin!'

'Just sit. This might help you. Come on.' He took Jake by the arm and guided him to the bed. Next, he went to the bookcase and picked up the photograph Jake had seen last time he was here — the portrait with the woman and two girls. He handed it to Jake.

'Do you know who these people are?'

'I thought they might be relations of yours.'

Ted nodded. 'My wife, actually. And my two daughters.'

Jake was shocked. He hadn't thought of

Ted having a wife — he seemed like someone who had been alone his whole life. Of course, Jessie had said she was his granddaughter and Cara his daughter, but he had decided early on this was just one of her lies. Besides, neither of the girls in the photo was Cara.

'What happened to them?'

'My wife left me, a long time ago,' said Ted. 'Then Cara and Jessie died.'

Jake started. He looked up, confused. Jessie was staring at him placidly.

'I don't understand,' he said.

'Well, I'll explain it to you, boy.' Ted sat heavily back in his chair. He stretched out his hand towards Jake, who handed the photo back to him. The old man started to talk as he stroked the glass of the portrait.

'When I was younger, about your dad's age, you wouldn't have recognised me. I was a law-yer. I lived in a big house, high up on the hills overlooking the sea. I wore smart suits every day, went to expensive restaurants. I defended big businesses, gave them legal advice, and they paid me far more than I was worth, I can tell you. I thought I was happy. I'd worked hard to get to that point. But I'll admit that I was lonely. Oh sure, there were women in my life, but I always felt a bit suspicious of them, thought they were only after my money.

'I bought a boat, the *Sea Mist*, which I kept in a special boat shed and launched down at Island Bay. Even though I was always working, any time I managed to steal was always spent in that boat. Powerful motor it had. I could blast out past the breakers and into the open sea, feel the wind on my face and forget about work. Don't get me wrong, I loved my job — the sense of power all that money gave me. The challenge of winning cases, especially if I suspected my client was in the wrong. I saved them so much money, they practically showered me with champagne. But deep down I had a cold feeling in my gut, and after each case it would take longer and longer in the boat for me to feel calm and clean again. And always, I went home to my huge empty house on the hill and I'd pour myself a glass of whiskey and sit alone on my deck, looking out at the sea. I got to realise that the huge gulf inside me was an absence of love.

'It was like Alice had heard my thoughts. One summer evening, after a gruelling day at work, I was in the boat, preparing to take it out to sea and forget my troubles. The tide was at its highest, about to turn. I saw something floating in the water. At first I thought it was a dead dog, but when I looked closer I saw that it was a perfectly preserved animal pelt. I fished it out and looked at it. It was a beautiful sealskin, reddish brown, but with silver flecks in it that caught the light as I turned it over in my hands. I was enchanted.

'I put it away in my hold, intending to take it home and keep it for my collection of curiosities.

'I'd only just made it past the breakers when the engine started to make a terrible graunching noise. I didn't want to risk being stranded out to sea, so I guided the *Sea Mist* back into shore, thinking I'd get a mechanic to look at her before I took her out again. The light had dimmed considerably, and as I bobbed towards the boat ramp, engine off, I heard a splashing beside me in the water. I looked down and saw a woman there, out for an evening swim. She had pale skin and huge dark eyes, and I couldn't take my eyes off her. Realising that I was staring, I thought it best to speak to her.

'"Hello," I said. "How's the water?"

'She took a moment to reply, just floating in the water, looking back at me. When she spoke it was as though her voice made a beeline for my heart.

'"Kind sir," she said, like something out of a fairy tale. "If you could please help me. I have lost my clothing. I came down to swim here and I fear that the tide rose higher than usual and the sea took it. I have been swimming around here for an hour or more, looking, and I am very tired."

'She was the most free and beautiful creature I'd ever seen, but the poor thing looked scared as well as tired, so I looked around for something to give her.

'"Here." I put a towel and a spare shirt and pants at the ladder, which I lowered into the water. Then I went and stood on the other side of the boat with my back to her.

'I heard her splashing out of the sea, her light footsteps on the deck, and when she announced that she was covered, I turned and I knew I'd found the love of my life. At the time I couldn't explain why I was so sure, and I didn't really want to know why. I just knew that from then on my life was going to change.

'Alice had the most profound effect on me. I saw my life for what it was — shallow and corrupt. I quit my job and sold my house, but I kept the *Sea Mist*. We lived for a long time on the proceeds of the house, and on the money I'd invested. We lived in a small cottage in Owhiro Bay, possibly even the house your father lives in now, who knows? I was very happy. I fished every day, and Alice was always waiting for me at home when I arrived. She fell pregnant and we had a beautiful daughter, Cara, and not long after that, another, Jessie. I thought I might die of happiness.

'But things were not quite right with Alice. While I was content just to have her by my side, her unhappiness grew clearer by the day. I'd come home and she'd have an exhausted, haunted look about her. Her feet were often cut and bruised, but when I asked her why, she'd brush me aside and say she'd fallen, or that she'd been gardening. I urged her to wear shoes, but she wouldn't.

'At nights I often found her standing at the open window, letting in the freezing wind, while she looked out to sea.

'Finally, she broke down one night and

told me what she was. A selkie — one of the seal-people. She'd shed her skin that day, and the tide had risen and taken it from the rocks, where it had floated my way. She told me that she only needed to find it and she could leave and be happy.

'But of course I didn't want her to leave. I had forgotten about the sealskin, and it had sat all those years in a box in the hold below deck. Alice had been in the boat, but she'd never guessed that the skin was right under her nose. I think the boat's proximity to the sea somehow masked the smell of it. After she'd told me her story, I held her in my arms for a long time, but I didn't tell her that it was me who was keeping her captive.

'She was growing sicker by the day, and yearned for the sea more and more. The girls were neglected. Often I'd come home and they'd be crying with hunger and I suspected she'd been leaving them alone while she went out walking, searching the streets and the water for her skin.

'One evening, I came home and she wasn't

there. The children had bloodied fingernails from trying to claw their way out of the locked house. They clung to me with fear and confusion when I opened the door and I saw them for what they were — they were as thin as flower stems and just as weak. I'd have to do something about it. I'd have to choose between my wife and my daughters.

'She arrived home in the middle of the night, drenched and clammy, but didn't seem to feel the cold. Her briny smell when she climbed into bed beside me was overpowering. She fell into an exhausted sleep and I knew what I had to do. I woke early, and, while she slept, went down to the *Sea Mist* to collect the skin.

'There it was, in its box where I'd left it all those years ago. I worried that it had been attacked by insects, that it'd fall apart when I lifted it, but it was as glossy and beautiful as the day I found it. When I took it from its box the smell — her smell, Alice's — was all around me.

'I brought the sealskin home. The children

were playing happily on the floor while she was in the kitchen, making them breakfast. She turned to greet me, a smile on her lips, but her face changed when she realised what I had in my arms. I don't know how, maybe it was the way her eyes grew and went black, but I sensed what was coming. I dropped the skin on the floor, picked up the children and all but tossed them into their room. I turned to face her as she threw her body against mine, shrieking.

'She nearly killed me. I'll say no more, but when she had finished with me, I could hardly walk or see. As I lay bleeding on the floor, she picked up the skin and ran from the house, ripping off her clothes as she went. By the time I'd dragged myself to the window and pulled myself to standing, she was a silky missile in the ocean, leaping and arcing, rippling the water. Then she disappeared.

'My heart and body were broken. I lay on the couch while the children called "Mummy, Mummy" around me, pleading for me to get up and look for her. Somehow I managed to get off the couch and feed them, put them to bed that evening, where they cried themselves to sleep. I hated myself then. It was all my fault. I'd unwittingly trapped Alice and now I was alone and my children motherless. She was a wild beast that should never have been tamed, and I blamed her for attacking me no more than I would blame a caged lion that turned on its trainer.

'I don't know how the girls knew, but it must have been in their blood. When I woke up the next morning, they were gone. They must have sensed what had happened to Alice, and had opened the front door and wandered down to the sea, looking for her. A neighbour found their little bodies washed up on the beach. They possessed neither a sealskin to transform them nor the ability to swim. They had tried to follow their mother and the sea had rejected them. I still wonder if she could have saved them, but perhaps she was already far away. I'll never know. I never saw her again.'

17

The sound of the sea rose up around them. Ted was staring at the photograph in his hands and Jessie was looking at Jake, as if waiting for him to speak. When it became clear that Ted had finished his story, Jake said to Jessie, 'You're not his granddaughter, are you?'

She shook her head — a little sadly, Jake thought. He looked around the room, and for the first time registered that with only one single bed, where did Jessie sleep when she stayed? That was one clue he'd missed. Now that he knew the truth for sure, that Ted wasn't really her grandfather, Jake knew she didn't sleep in the hut at all.

Ted looked up. 'There have been many Jessies, my boy. And Caras. They don't replace my daughters, but if I can look out for them, even just while they're small — give them clothes to wear, offer them some protection from humans — it takes away the worst of the guilt. And I can pretend for a while that my girls never left. This Cara first came to me last year — she was the same age Jessie is now. She was a sweet girl. Seals grow up a lot faster than humans, so she's an adult now and I'd thought we wouldn't be seeing her again. But she was drawn back. And this is the first time in all these years that one of my girls has lost their skins. I feared for her, and for the poor sod who had found it, but there wasn't much I could do. Cara and your dad are both wrapped up in the enchantment now. Nobody can reason with either of them.'

'But why do they come to land and shed their skins?' asked Jake. 'Nobody's explained it to me.'

Ted sighed, then shook his head. 'Who knows, lad? Maybe it's loneliness and sorrow that brings them out of the sea. Mine . . .' He hung his head, as though ashamed. '. . . and now your dad's. I don't know. Maybe it's just because they can. I'm sure they couldn't explain it to you any more than I could.'

Could it be true? Was Dad so lonely that he had drawn a woman from a seal? And Jessie: was she just one in a line of selkie-children brought out of the sea by poor Ted's suffering? Jake couldn't believe that. She was too curious, too much her own person. He remembered what his dad had said, that night by the fire. 'Wouldn't you? Just to see what it was like?'

Jake looked at Jessie again. 'Would you have ever told me? That you're . . .' He couldn't finish his own sentence, and Jessie didn't react. It didn't matter what she was. She was his friend, that was enough.

Jake fell silent again, thinking. Things were even scarier than he'd realised. Ted's limp, and his badly scarred eyelid, were all because of his selkie wife. Dad was in danger — two-fold. If Cara found out he was hiding her skin — wherever it was! — she could hurt him, badly, even if he gave it back to her voluntarily. On the other hand, if Jake's dad managed to keep the sealskin from her for long enough, he and Cara might have children, and Cara could die and leave him heartbroken, or worse, their children could follow their mother into the sea and drown.

Jake had to admit to himself that even though he'd been urging Dad to give back the skin for his own good, it had really been for selfish reasons. Jake had been jealous. He didn't want his dad to start another family. But after Ted's story, Jake realised things were far more complicated than that.

With a start, something came to him that had been nagging him all this time — his dad could end up like Ted. Alone, sad, and slightly crazy.

Then another terrible thought struck him. Dad had insisted that Cara would stay with him even if he gave her back the skin. What if he decided to test his theory? Jake had to get back home, fast, to make sure he didn't. He jumped to his feet.

'I have to go,' he said.

Ted stood up. 'You know what you have to do now? Where to look?'

'I think I have an idea. But even if I find it and give it back, won't she be angry?'

Jessie piped up. She practically rolled her eyes, as if Jake was just a silly child. 'You do not give it back to her, Jake. You put it back where you found it, then the spell will be broken and she can leave.'

'Will you come with me? Help me look for it?'

'No. She will get suspicious. You must do this on your own.' She sounded to Jake like a grown-up in a child's body. All this time he had thought of her as a little kid, but she was quickly becoming far wiser than he could hope to be in his lifetime.

He opened the front door cautiously, trying to make as little noise as possible. All was quiet. They must be out, thought Jake, but when he entered the living room, there was his father, sitting at the dining table, staring out the window. He was hunched over, wearing his holey black fishing jersey and faded brown corduroy pants. His whiskers were starting to resemble a proper beard. It was happening already — he was already starting to look like Ted. A younger version, but Ted all the same, like the Ted in the photograph.

There was no sign of Cara. Jake dared to hope that she had left, and everything was fine.

'Hi, Dad.'

Dad turned his head slowly and looked at him. His eyes were glassy and it was as though it took him a second to recognise his own son. 'Oh, Jake.' His voice was listless. 'You're back.'

Jake sat down opposite him. 'Where's Cara?' he asked.

'She's gone out for a walk.'

Looking for the skin, thought Jake, but didn't say so. 'And what are you doing?' Jake was surprised his dad wasn't taking the opportunity to work on his book.

'I'm waiting for her.'

This was worse than Jake thought. Dad was completely under the selkie's spell. He was like an empty shell; or a child waiting for its mother, not knowing how to entertain itself. But as Jake sat with him, the colour slowly came back into his father's cheeks, the life back into his eyes. Suddenly Dad's eyes opened wide.

'Jake!' he said, as if only just noticing him. 'How's your day going? Do you want some lunch?' He stood up and started moving towards the kitchen. Jake realised one important fact: his own presence was somehow diluting Cara's spell. There was hope after all that they could fight this thing. Ted had been alone, with nobody to distract him from his enchantment. Perhaps things were going to be different this time.

'We have to talk,' said Jake.

Dad stopped. 'Okay,' he said, and sat down again.

Jake told him what had happened to Ted, in much fewer words. For the first time, his dad looked as though he might be listening. But still, he refused to believe that what he had with Cara was anything but love.

'I'm sorry that happened to Ted,' he said. 'It must be horrible to lose your children like that. If anything ever happened to you, I don't know what I'd do.' He grabbed Jake's hand across the table. 'But, mate, this isn't what's happening here. I'm sure Ted's wife just left him and he was so sad he just made up the story to make himself feel better.'

'Dad!' Jake shouted in frustration. 'Don't you see? We have to let Cara have her skin back, and we can't let her know we've had it!'

But his father wasn't looking at him any more. He was staring at the doorway to the living room. Jake turned, his stomach a pit of dread, knowing what he would see. Cara leant against the doorframe, listening.

'My skin is here?' Cara's voice stayed calm, but she began advancing slowly towards them. Jake found himself shrinking away from her. She radiated a coldness that he could feel on his skin. 'Where is it?'

Neither Jake nor his father said anything. Dad was staring at her, mesmerised, just the way Jake had stared at her that day in Ted's cottage.

And then she began to change. It was her eyes at first — they seemed to grow in her face. Her pupils expanded in her irises, then her irises expanded and covered the whites of her eyes. Jake was cold with fear, and Dad gasped. But still neither of them spoke. They were both in danger, and yet Jake couldn't move.

'Where is it?' Her voice rose in pitch and volume and filled the air around them. She pulled her lips back in a grimace. Her teeth were small and pointed. She looked wildly around the room. Then she ran to the couch and started tearing at it with her bare hands. Within seconds the cushions were shredded, their stuffing floating through the air. She whirled around the room, throwing all the books from their shelves, upturning the coffee table. Next, she swept into the kitchen, and the sound of smashing glass and crockery rumbled through the house.

With Cara in the next room, Jake came to his senses and jumped to his feet. He grabbed his father's arm. 'Come on, we have to get out of here! If she finds it, she'll kill us!'

But his father wrenched his arm free. 'Don't be ridiculous,' he said. 'She's just a bit upset, that's all. I'll tell her you were joking, that it was just a game.' Jake could barely hear him over the sound of splintering wood as Cara tore the kitchen apart.

'Dad!' Jake shouted. Suddenly, silence spilled from the kitchen. Cara appeared in the doorway. When she spoke, her voice was gravelly and low, a mixture of human voice and animal growl. Her eyes were black coals throbbing in her face. They pulsed with an unearthly light.

'My love,' she said to Dad. 'Why do you keep that little room above the house locked? What is inside that you do not want me to see?'

'It's just my workroom, Cara,' Dad said. 'My computer's in there. I keep the door locked so it doesn't get stolen.' Jake could see that the enchantment was slipping again. For the first time, he saw fear on his father's face. Dad glanced at him. When Cara disappeared from view and they heard the back door open, Dad whispered urgently: 'Go. The boat. It's in the boat.'

It was as Jake suspected. He lunged for the hall and was out the front door in seconds.

As he tore through the gate, he turned to see the door to Dad's writing room falling off its hinges; Cara had pulled it off with her bare hands. The next moment the computer crashed through the window and clattered onto the roof of the cottage, and all of his father's papers exploded into the air and swirled around like a snowstorm. He only hoped that Dad could calm her down once she had finished, convince her that what she had overheard was indeed a joke, and that she wouldn't turn her fury onto him. He ran as though his father's life depended on it, because it did.

18

He had forgotten about the padlock on the boat locker but there it was, staring him in the face. Jake pulled at the doors desperately but they stayed shut, rocking slightly on their hinges. The wind had picked up and it threw grit in his eyes, making them water, mixing with tears of frustration. There was only one thing for it — he'd have to try and break the doors down. He looked around but there was nobody else about to help him, which was probably just as well; he'd have a hard time convincing them he wasn't just a delinquent breaking into a boat locker.

He picked up a rock from the beach, light enough to lift, but heavy enough to use as a sledgehammer. Bang! He brought it down on the top of the padlock, scraping his knuckles in the process. Nothing. He did it again, taking more skin off, but urgency made his hands numb to the pain. This time, he'd loosened it a little. Just one more . . . bang!

The screws came out of the soft, splintered wood and he was able to wrench and twist until the lock came away properly. He was in.

It didn't take him long to find the skin — in such a small boat there were few places to hide anything. The rubbish sack he'd hidden the skin in himself was tucked into the bow, under the anchor and chain. He put his hand inside it to check, and when he touched the soft fur, the smell of it enveloped him. For a moment he felt dizzy and closed his eyes. It was as if Cara was all around him; he felt her breath in his ear, and his heart suddenly swelled with warmth for her. A thought jolted him: what on earth was he doing? Returning the skin to the cave banishing Cara from their lives forever — is that really what he wanted? If he kept it here, hidden in the little boat, then his dad would be happy. He had seen the light in his face when she was around. And Cara could be like another mother for Jake — together, they could be a family. Wouldn't that be nice?

Suddenly he thought he felt the skin move, and he tore his hand away. In that very moment, another vision popped into his head: Jessie's face, telling him to be brave, and then — oddly, for he hadn't thought of him much — his brother Davey. There was already a real family waiting for him back in Auckland: his mother, Greg, and his little brother. He and Dad were a real family too, in their own way, no matter what. Keeping Cara bound to them would not make them any more of a family than they already were. In fact, when she was around, Jake was shut out.

He would have to be careful. Now he was in possession of the skin, he was falling under its spell again. He closed the bag and tied a tight knot at the top. Then he crawled out of the locker.

What was he going to do now? He couldn't risk taking it back home and giving it to Cara; even walking past the house carried the danger of being seen and intercepted by her. And it was a long walk from Island Bay to the cave at Red Rocks. It could take him the rest of the day. But that would be too long. Who knew what state she was in and whether Dad had managed to calm her down?

There was only one option, one that scared Jake, but that he knew was his only choice.

He didn't know where he found the strength, especially with his bruised wrist, but he tugged at the little boat with his skinny arms, jerking it across the sand and down to the water. The beach was deserted, which was highly unusual — often there were families playing in the sand, or people walking their dogs. It was as if the whole world was staying away, determined to neither help nor hinder him in his task.

He attached the outboard motor as he'd watched his father do it, strapped on his life jacket, and launched himself and the dinghy into the water, rowing out into the depths. The wind was making the sea choppy but he kept his balance as he put down the oars and pulled the cord of the motor once, then again. It grumbled into life. Jake wished that his dad had had it fixed since the last time they'd been out in the boat, but with all the time he'd been spending with Cara, he wouldn't have had time. The boat and its motor were the only way though, so Jake set out, now too fast, now too slow, trying to catch a feel for the throttle and fighting the fear in his belly, expecting the motor to fail at any moment as it had on their fishing trip.

He couldn't stay too close to the shore, as there

were unseen rocks that could tear the bottom of the boat. And yet he worried that the further out he went, the more the pull of the tide might send him out to sea. He manoeuvred out of Island Bay between the island and the empty beach. Cold spray flew into his face and he had a moment of exhilaration, of feeling alone and free. He imagined keeping the nose of the boat southwards and chasing the ferry he could see in the distance, all the way to the South Island and away from the disaster he had created.

The engine hiccupped and lost power for a second, snapping Jake out of his reverie, but thankfully it soon roared again. He checked the shore to see how far he had come. He had left Island Bay and its bobbing fishing boats behind and was now turning the boat to the west. Away from the shelter of the island the waves grew larger; they slapped the side of the boat and he was soon soaked to the skin. His hands on the throttle stick became numb but he didn't dare take them off to shake the feeling back into them.

He felt he was going quite fast, and yet the shore crawled by, along with the lonely cars in the café car park, the flax flowers that bent in the breeze. The sound of the motor buzzed in his brain, driving him on.

He closed his eyes for a moment. More than anything, he wished he could lie down and go to sleep, to pull warm, dry covers over his head and wake up to a bright day with no trouble. When he opened them again, the shore had receded, and now he was travelling past the bite of Owhiro Bay, with its rocky sand, the gulls crowded around, looking out at him. He searched for his father's house — there it was, sitting idle and quiet, with no sign of life. Jake shuddered. Wait! A figure stood on a rock, looking out to sea, watching him. He recognised Cara's bright red cardigan — but where was Dad? What had she done with him? He held his breath, expecting her to start moving, to run along the beach, or worse, to dive into the water and come for him. But it was as if her feet were part of the rock on which she stood.

Only her hair moved in the wind. Perhaps she could sense her skin was on the move, that Dad no longer had it in his possession, but she didn't follow, only stood with her body straining towards the sea, waiting. Something behind her caught his eye and his stomach leapt inside him — Dad? — but it was the flapping of a curtain that had slipped loose through the broken window of the office. It was as though it were waving him on, urging him to go faster.

On he went, past the line of houses with their faces turned to the ocean. The car park for Red Rocks came into view. He was going to make it. He was nearly there. Still further, with the great grey cliffs looking blankly at him. He wondered how he must look to anyone standing up there — a small speck on the vast ocean, probably, with a tiny smudge of bright yellow for a life jacket. Insignificant.

There was Ted's cabin. The smoke spiralled up before disappearing, stolen by the wind. A figure stood in front of the little shack. It was

Ted: he raised a hand high and then waved, painting huge strokes with his arms. There was no sign of Jessie. Jake waved back, bolstered by the old man's faith in him. But as he did so, his cold hand slipped on the throttle and the boat jumped forward like a mullet being chased by a kahawai. He fell back and banged his head on the motor, losing his grip completely. The engine died and Jake was enveloped by the sound of water, all around, clawing at the boat. The wind whistled in his wet ears. He sat up. 'No, no, no,' he said quietly to himself. He pulled the starter cord. Nothing. He tried again. And again, and again until his arm ached with the effort. He was being pulled further away from the shore by the tide and if he let himself drift any more he'd be gone in no time.

Jake picked up the oars and, with shaking hands, jiggled the rowlocks into place. Then he began to row. He had made it this far, most of the way, now he had to rely on his physical strength to get him there. His wrist was still sore, and doubt crowded into his mind — how on earth would he do it? He'd only learned to row last summer, had only just moved beyond turning the boat in circles and having no control over its direction. Plus, he was weak. Those older boys had spotted that fact a mile off, had pushed him around like a dandelion in the wind, and he had let them. How could he gather the strength to get him the last part of the way?

19

All Jake had to focus on was the steady pull, pull, pull on the oars, and he surprised himself by cutting through the water like a blade. His arms and shoulders strained with the effort, but he didn't give up. Every now and then he turned to look at Red Rocks, waiting for him. At first, they seemed to be getting no nearer, but as the sweat began to run into his eyes, he turned again and there they were, blazing red. All that was left to do was negotiate the submerged rocks and bring the boat into shore.

Jake stopped rowing. He was breathing hard and all he wanted to do was rest, but he was so close he couldn't give up. The waves buffeted the boat around as if it were made of paper. Jake pointed the nose of the dinghy in between two rocks and pulled on one oar, then the other until he was safely through. The water was thick with clumps of kelp, and it parted sluggishly to let him through. He stood up for just a second, to scan the rocks for seals, but they were empty. As he lowered himself back into his seat, a wave picked up the boat and tossed it sideways. There was an almighty scraping sound, and the tearing of wood. It was just as he had feared would happen: he had hit a rock, and the boat was stuck fast. Water began to lap at his feet as it filled up, and he was going to have to act fast. He had his life jacket on; he could do it. He would swim the rest of the way.

He stood up, crouching for stability, with the rubbish bag tucked under his arm, and stared into the surging sea. The water in the boat covered his sneakers now. He took some deep breaths to try and calm himself; he was shaking uncontrollably, and not just from the cold that caused his limbs to stiffen in pain. It was now or never.

Jake jumped. He had thought the life jacket would keep him above the surface, but the weight of his body dragged him under for a moment before he popped up, coughing. The shock of the cold had made him inhale as he hit the water, and he panicked, nearly dropping the sealskin. He clung to the boat to get his bearings, and to gather his courage. His heart was still beating fast. It was time to let go and swim.

It was more difficult than he imagined, because he only had one useable arm. He floated on his side, with the sealskin clutched under his left arm, while he crawled with his right arm and frog-kicked his legs. Something touched him under the water and he gave an involuntary yell, but it was just the slimy tentacles of kelp, which felt as though they were trying to wrap themselves around him and pull him under. He kicked himself free. He was so tired, felt so desperate, as he rose and fell helplessly with the swell of the sea. Suddenly a wave broke and crashed over him, slamming him into a rock. His mouth filled with salty water and pain rushed up his shoulder. He couldn't go on. He used the last of his strength to crawl up onto the rock, where he lay, panting and coughing, fighting tears. He felt pretty sure that he was going to die here. He lay, listening to the pounding surf and, high above him, the keening of seagulls. The sun came out from behind a cloud and the warmth of it hit his back. He opened his eyes and stared at the rubbish sack. Beads of water sparkled on it. He was so close he could almost see his face in each one, if he just closed one eye and focused . . .

*

He must have dozed off. He was woken by a dog nudging his face, breathing its hot breath on him. He pushed it away. The rubbish sack was a comfortable pillow under his head, and he just wanted to sleep for five more minutes. But the dog was insistent. Its whiskers tickled his face. He pushed it away one last time and sat up. He had forgotten where he was for a moment.

There was no dog. Instead, he found himself looking into the dark, liquid eyes of a seal, twitching its whiskery snout. He lurched back and nearly tipped himself into the water. The seal turned and dived below the surface. Jake stood up and looked at how far he had to go — he was much closer than he had thought. The clouds had stolen the sun again and the sea was a sullen grey. He picked up the sealskin, wincing with the pain in his shoulder, and lowered himself gingerly into the sea. He hadn't meant to rest, and he didn't know how long he had been asleep — probably only a few minutes — but it was enough. He felt ready to go again. The water became sheltered and calm as he got closer to shore, and soon he felt solid ground under his feet. Relief swept through him. He was safe.

The wind was sharp when he took his life jacket off, but it restricted his movement on land, so it had to go. He located the slit in the rock, and scrambled to the entrance of the cave. He stopped and looked around. There were no seals on the rocks nearby, but when he looked further out he saw dark shapes bobbing in the surging water, and he knew he was being watched. He shivered.

Jake dropped to his knees and held the bag with the sealskin in front of him as he crawled into the hole. He inched forward bit by bit, with the rocks digging into his knees. All his senses were alert — if there was something, or someone, in there already, he was going to just drop the bag and make himself scarce. But he got to end of the tunnel and heard and felt nothing. It was warm in the cave, despite his wet clothes. He felt faint and thirsty and wished he had food or water with him.

In the darkness, the sealskin slipped out of the bag. He held it tightly, buried his fingers in the damp fur. He could not bring himself to put it down. Instead, he hugged it fiercely and thought of Cara. Her face appeared in his mind, so beautiful; he could see every feature as clearly as if she stood in front of him now.

It's just the spell, he thought, and fought it with every instinct he possessed, even though the enchantment was telling him to hold tight and never let it go. But he managed, by sheer force of will, to put the skin down, and he gasped as his hands came away; it was if he was tearing off his own skin. And as he did so, a ripple went through the air around him, like a great sigh, and he turned his face to the light outside, and knew that he and his father were free. He only needed to back carefully out of the cave and return home.

As he emerged, blinking, into the light, he froze: he heard voices, laughter, and something else, a groaning. A seal! He crouched where he was, hiding from it. The last thing he wanted to meet coming out from the cave was a seal. Then a stone thudded down next to him, narrowly missing his shoulder. Slowly, he rose up to peer over the rocks. He stopped. The back of a small seal appeared before him. It was sitting upright, swaying back and forth, clearly distressed. And then he saw why. He recognised the hulking shape in the brown hoodie and the blonde spiky hair: jeering at the seal and throwing stones were the two boys who had stolen his bike. The seal looked mad, but as it advanced to defend itself, Mark, the bigger of the boys, threw a fist-sized rock, which hit the seal on the head. Stunned, the animal staggered backwards.

Jake couldn't stop himself. 'Hey!' The seal turned and looked at him, just as another smaller stone glanced off its neck. Jake jumped up from his hiding place and ran on his tired, quivering legs, past the seal and right up to the two boys. 'Stop it!' he shouted. 'You're hurting it!'

The boys looked surprised to see him; they'd obviously thought they were alone. They smelled of cigarette smoke, and their hands and faces were grubby. Mark's pale cheeks flushed when Jake approached, and he turned to Dan. They nudged each other and forced laughs.

'You're like a bad smell, you are, popping up all over the place.' Dan narrowed his already small eyes so they nearly disappeared into his white lashes. 'What are you going to do about it?'

Jake didn't know what he was going to do about it, but he planted his feet firmly and stood between the boys and the seal. When Mark bent to pick up another stone, Jake lunged at him and knocked it from his hand.

'Oi!' shouted the boys in unison. Dan stepped forward and pushed Jake hard, toppling him backwards. His tailbone landed sharply on the rocks and the pain winded him for a moment. He felt sick to the stomach. But he pulled himself to his feet and resumed his defiant position — feet apart, arms folded. His shoulder still hurt and his wrist throbbed from where he had fallen yesterday, but he dampened it all down.

'I said, leave it alone.' He felt shaky inside, but his voice did not betray him and it sounded calm and firm.

Dan picked up another rock, and Jake was sure he was going to be the target this time, but Mark caught his friend by the arm. 'Come on,' he said. 'This guy's a loser anyway.' Jake thought he had intimidated the boy, but he soon saw what he was looking at — the wheel of Jake's bike was poking out from behind a rock. Dan shoved Jake again on his way past, but this time Jake didn't fall down. The boys swaggered over to where the bike lay and gave two vicious kicks to the wheels, breaking the spokes with a crunch. Then they seemed to change their minds and picked it up. Together the boys made off with Jake's precious bike again, whooping as they ran.

20

As soon as the boys were gone, Jake turned to look at the seal. It lay on its side, breathing heavily. He crept up to get a closer look. It eyed him back and seemed to sigh. Its head was smeared with blood. He knew this was the same seal that had woken him on the rock, and he would bet that it was also the same seal that had guided him and his dad back to shore that day.

There wasn't much he could do for it, and

an injured animal could be dangerous, so he should keep his distance. But this seal wasn't like any others. Jake put his hand gently on its side, which rose and fell.

'I'll get help,' he promised. The seal looked him in the eyes and blinked, and Jake took it as a sign that it understood him. Then he ran. His whole back stung but he pushed through it. He stumbled several times and grazed his hands once, but each time he fell, he picked himself up and ran on.

He banged on Ted's door. He knew before he got to the hut that Jessie wouldn't be there, but a small part of him hoped that he was wrong about so many things. When he stumbled inside, he could see that Ted was alone.

'You made it! Well done, young fella,' said Ted. But then his face changed when he saw Jake's; Ted caught Jake as he sank to his knees.

Jake knelt, panting, trying to catch his breath enough to speak.

'There's a seal . . . it's hurt . . . some boys . . .

hurt it. I think it's . . .'

Ted looked grave. Jake wasn't going to say what was on his mind, but he could tell that Ted knew exactly what he was thinking.

'Where is it?' Ted gripped him by both shoulders.

'Near the cave where the sealskin . . .'

Ted jumped to his feet, surprisingly agile for his age. He made for the door, then hesitated. He crossed back and picked up some clothes. 'You stay here, boy. You've done your bit.' Then he was gone.

Jake sat on the floor for what felt like an eternity, too sore to move. He managed to crawl over to the sink and pull himself up to grab a glass of water. He guzzled it down, spilling half of it down his front before pouring another and drinking that too. Then he sat down on the bed to wait.

He must have fallen asleep. The next thing he knew, he was lying on his side on the bed and the front door was being kicked open. Ted staggered in, red-faced and sweating. In his arms he carried a child — no, not a child, a teenage girl, who clung to his neck and buried her face in his shoulder.

'Move!' he barked, and Jake sprang to his feet. Ted laid the girl carefully on the bed.

It was Jessie, as Jake knew it would be. She wore a baggy pair of shorts and the holey black jersey Ted had taken as he left. Except it wasn't the Jessie he knew — she looked too old, at least fourteen. Her legs were longer, ganglier, and her hair spread about her like seaweed. It shone with congealed blood from the cut on her head. Her eyes were closed.

Jake stood by with his hand over his mouth. 'Will she be all right?' he muttered through his fingers.

Ted said nothing. He clattered around by the sink, pulling out a bottle of disinfectant and slopping it into a bowl of water. Then he looked around the room until he spied the clean towel on the drying rack. He tossed it to Jake. 'Rip this up.'

Jake did as he was told. He tore at the towel until it was nothing but little squares. He poured all of his anxiety into the task, and hardly took his eyes off Jessie's face as she twitched and made small moaning sounds on the bed.

Ted pulled up a chair next to the bed and tenderly dabbed at Jessie's wound. Jessie opened her eyes and winced. She tried to sit up but Ted gently held her down.

'You just stay there, missy,' he said.

'I am fine,' she said. She looked intently into Ted's eyes. 'Really.' There was a force in her voice Jake had not heard before. Ted removed his hand from her shoulder and she sat up.

'Jake,' she said, and smiled weakly. 'I am so glad to see you.'

Jake felt shy suddenly. He nodded and felt himself grow pink. Despite her injury, and her baggy old clothes, she looked beautiful. Was this a trick? Was he falling under the spell of the selkie again?

'Come here, please.'

Ted stood up and made way for Jake, who sat down in the chair at the head of the bed. Jessie took his hand, and Jake knew this was no spell — after all, her skin must be safely hidden away. What he felt for her was real. 'Thank you,' she whispered. Jake nodded again. He flinched when she squeezed his hand.

'Oh,' she said. 'You are hurt.' She examined his scraped palms, but they were the least of his pains: his shoulder, his wrist, his tailbone and legs were all bruised and aching.

'No,' he said. 'It's nothing. Are you all right?'

She put a hand to her head. The bleeding had stopped. 'Just bruised. You are very brave.'

Jake pulled away from her, standing up and moving to the window. He couldn't quite acknowledge what she had said to him. Part of him still wanted to hold on to the belief that he had simply stopped some boys from hurting a seal, but that the seal was just that — an animal. That somehow Jessie had been watching him, and that was how she knew he had helped. But she no longer hid the fact she was a selkie just like Cara. There was so much he wanted to ask her. What was it like to be a seal? How did it feel to inhabit the body of a different creature? But now was not the time: he'd ask her another day.

He said nothing and stared out the window. He could see his bike lying on the road, its handlebars twisted and broken. So the boys had abandoned it and run off. It would be a long walk home with his aching bones, but he knew he had to set off soon. He didn't know if his father was hurt or even alive at all, but it was too much for him to contemplate right now, and he pushed the thought away.

He saw a movement out of the corner of his eye, and when he looked he saw a figure gliding over the stones. It was Cara. She was wearing the old overcoat and her feet were bare again. Her face was intent, looking out towards Red Rocks. As she passed the house, she turned her head and saw Jake at the window. Jake stiffened, unsure how she would react to him, but she smiled at him and raised a hand. Jake raised his also.

'How does she know? You didn't get the chance to tell her.'

Ted came and stood behind him and they watched her walking away. 'The spell's broken now. As soon as you put it back, she had nothing keeping her at your house. You did a good job today, boy.'

'But she found out.' Jake felt ashamed. 'She overheard us talking. She tore the place apart. And I just left him there. What if she's killed him?'

Ted put his hand on Jake's unhurt shoulder and squeezed firmly. 'I have a feeling he's all right, but you should go, just to make sure. You go. I'll stay here with Jessie.'

Jake groaned. All he wanted to do was lie down, but he knew he had to make one last effort. Despite Ted's assurances, he was terrified about what he would find when he got home.

21

It was almost dark by the time he reached his father's house. The clouds had all cleared and the wind died away to a whisper. A few stars were beginning to show, sparse sprinklings of light in the sky. Jake dragged his aching body through the gate but with a last burst of energy ran up the steps to where the front door stood slightly ajar.

'Dad!' he called. Panic set in when there was

no answer. He ran into the living room, where it looked as though a hurricane and an earthquake had struck at once: upturned and broken dining chairs lurched drunkenly, books were tipped all over the floor, dents pocked the walls where hardbacks had been flung. Stuffing from the couch cushions covered the floor like candyfloss. Jake stuck his head in the kitchen, just to make sure it was empty, and was greeted by the smell of vinegar and spices from the smashed bottles and jars that littered the floor. There was no sign of his father.

Forgetting the pain in his body, he ran outside, his ears ringing. He glanced up at the shed, but something drew him away from the house, some instinct he didn't know he had. He crossed the road blindly and ran down to the beach. In the dying light, which streaked the sky with orange and indigo, he scanned the sea and the beach. As the darkness crept around him, he saw a shape on a patch of sand between some rocks. Jake stared harder. It looked like a log at first, then a seal, and he took a step back. He mustn't disturb it. But as his eyes adjusted to the failing light, he saw the shape on the beach was not a seal at all. It was too small, not bulky enough. It was a human, lying in the damp sand left behind by the tide.

'Dad!' Jake's chest felt as if it would explode. He ran. Tears stung his cheeks. He threw himself in the sand beside the body, which lay on its front, clothes soaked through, hair wet. It was his father all right, but he was as still as the rocks, and so cold. Jake yanked his shoulder, but Dad's big body was so heavy he couldn't shift it. He braced his legs in the sand and threw all his weight into it. This was harder than anything he'd had to do today, and Jake felt small and weak and desperate. But with a final shove, he managed to heave his father over onto his back. Even in the weak light Jake could see the blue lips, though half the face was gritty with wet sand. Dad's eyes were closed, his mouth slightly open, his face shockingly pale against the stringy hair that stuck to his forehead and the dark, damp beard. A long scratch travelled down one cheek.

'Dad!' he screamed, and shook him, but there was no response — the eyes remained resolutely shut. The light was draining from the beach and his father was being swallowed by the night.

Jake sat down beside him and let the tears come. Into his mind an image formed, of two small girls lying in this very spot, drowned by the sea that had welcomed their mother into its cold arms. He could see them so clearly, their thin, pale limbs in white nightdresses. And now, all these years later, his father lay here, on the same coarse sand. Ted had tried to warn him with his story, and Jake had worked so hard to save his father, pushing himself further than he ever thought was possible, but in the end, it was for nothing. He had failed. Everything was his fault, and now his father was surely dead. Grief pressed down onto his shoulders like a physical force, and he lay back on the wet sand. If only there was some way he could bring him back. He would give any part of himself just to see his father stand up and walk away.

He rolled over and put his head on his father's chest, smelt damp wool and salt, touched a cold hand. Suddenly, the body beneath him heaved. Dad's lungs filled with air, a great noisy gasp of it, and his chest expanded beneath Jake's cheek. Jake sat up and looked into the staring, wild eyes of his father, barely visible now in the dark.

'Jake?' gasped Dad. He only managed the one word before he started coughing. He rolled onto his side, doubled over and coughed and coughed until Jake was sure he would cough up his lungs. But soon he was quiet and still.

'It's me,' said Jake. 'I'm here.' His father's arms coiled around him, pulling him down onto his chest and squeezing. He felt the relief in his father's touch — the same relief that was now flooding through him.

'Oh, thank God,' Dad said. 'I thought you were dead.'

'You thought I was dead?' Jake was confused. Things were the wrong way around. It was his father who had lain, corpse-like, in the sand, not him. He sat up. He grabbed both of his father's hands, and just managed to pull him to a sitting position. Dad breathed heavily, one arm around Jake's shoulders.

'What happened?' asked Dad. 'Where are we?'

'We're just on the beach. Don't you remember?'

Dad groaned. 'Not really. Bits. Help me up.'

Together they got him to his shaky feet, and he stood, swaying for a minute.

'I thought you were dead,' said Jake. 'I thought you'd drowned.'

Dad said nothing, just nodded and leant on Jake as he started shuffling back towards the house. It was a slow journey, and Jake felt he might be crushed by his father's weight with every step. The house was dark, and when Jake flicked on the living room light, the harshness of it glanced off the carnage. Dad gasped, as though seeing it for the first time. He collapsed on the torn couch, shivering.

'I'll get a blanket,' Jake said. 'You're freezing.' When he came back, his father looked so small. Jake had always thought of his dad as a tall man, with legs that could take mountains in one stride, and yet here he sat looking tiny and, yes, weak. This was perhaps the biggest shock of all.

But he was alive. Apart from the long scratch down his cheek, and his skin blue with damp and cold, he looked physically unharmed. Jake put the blanket over him, then sat down next to him on the wrecked couch. Without its cushions, the springs dug into his backside. Dad's arm came around him, holding him tight. He seemed dazed, confused; Jake wasn't sure how much he knew or remembered.

'Are you okay?' he asked.

'She's gone, mate,' said Dad. 'She's gone and left me.'

'Yeah,' said Jake. 'I know.'

They sat in silence. Jake looked around the room at the chaos.

'What happened?' he asked. 'After I left?'

Dad turned and looked at him. His eyes were glassy again, as though he couldn't focus on him properly. 'I'm not sure,' he said. 'It's all a bit of a blur. Like I was drunk.' He was still shivering with the cold.

'What can you remember?'

'I managed to calm her down a bit, after she trashed the office. Not before she gave me this though.' He laid a finger gently on the scratch on his face. 'I told her you were just a silly kid playing a game, that you didn't know what you were saying. But not long after you left, she just pushed me aside and went and stood on the beach, looking out to sea. I left her there for a bit, I don't know how long for. That part's a bit fuzzy. Truth was, I was scared of her. Did you see her face? Her eyes?'

Jake nodded. He wondered if he had

unlocked the spell by touching the sealskin when he first got to the boat, and if that was the point at which Cara had broken away from his father, shutting him out. If he hadn't opened the bag, who knows what would have happened?

'After a bit, I went down to see her, but she just stood there, looking west, towards the rocks. I took her hand, tried to get her to come inside, but she was cold and hard, like a statue. I don't know what I did after that. But one thing I do remember: just before she left, there was this sound. It sounded like you, Jake, like you'd let out a huge sigh, but it was all around us. I looked for you, but you weren't here. And soon after that, she came back into the house. I thought she'd come back to me, but she said nothing, just changed into her dirty old clothes and walked out. She didn't even say goodbye, but I knew it was over before she'd even set foot out the door.

'After she left, I sat there for I don't know how long. It was like the world had stopped. Then there was a knock at the door. It was one of the local fisherman. He told me he'd seen my boat, smashed on the rocks with nobody inside it.

'I should have done something then, called a search party or something, but I wasn't myself, mate.' He hung his head, ashamed. 'This sounds crazy, but I thought I felt the sea calling me. Something told me that I could go after Cara, and find you, if I just went into the sea. I don't remember anything after that. Just you waking me up on the beach. I'm so sorry, Jake. I wasn't trying to drown myself, I promise.'

Jake nodded. 'I know. It's okay.'

Dad shook his head. 'I tell you what, buddy, there's been something weird going on here. And I don't know why, or what you did, but I feel like I owe you my life.'

'It was the sealskin. I found it, and I put it back.'

Dad opened his mouth, as if to speak, then closed it. He sighed and shrugged. 'I don't think I want to know. We're safe, that's all that matters.'

But Jake knew that he was lying — their safety wasn't all that mattered. He could see it in his father's slumped shoulders, his hollow eyes: he was upset that Cara had gone, and he was going to be upset for some time to come. Not just because of the enchantment: Dad had liked Cara before he knew about the power of the skin. The spell had intensified his feelings, made them irrational, but for a few days, Dad had held out a real hope that he had found someone to love.

'You'll meet someone else,' said Jake. His father just smiled a sad smile.

22

A hammering sound was coming from outside the window. In his bed, Jake bolted upright. *Cara*. Was she banging to get in, to claim her skin?

But when he squinted into the late morning light, the events of the day before came back and he sighed. Not Cara then. He was exhausted and his whole body ached, but he dragged himself to the window and looked out. Dad was up by his writing shed, hammering a piece of plywood over the broken glass.

Jake called out to him, and Dad waved and smiled. The haunted look was gone from his face, but Jake had a feeling that it was tucked away just out of sight, and would never be far from the surface. His father looked strong again in a singlet and jeans with his leather tool belt around his waist. Perhaps it was the fact that Dad's face was clean-shaven, making him younger, more himself, that made Jake think his old dad was looking back at him.

'Better get a move on,' Dad called. 'You've got a plane to catch at lunchtime!'

Jake groaned and turned back to his room. He found his suitcase and threw as many clothes and books as he could find into it, then went in search of breakfast.

Dad had obviously been up for some time. The stuffing had been squeezed back into the couch cushions, the books and newspapers picked up and put back on their shelves or stacked neatly on the floor.

In the kitchen, a small sliver of glass pierced one of his bare feet, and the floor was sticky and damp, but other than that the broken glass and crockery had been swept away. The cupboard doors had either been screwed back on or taken away completely, revealing empty, clean shelves. It was as if his father had tried to scrub away the memory of what Cara had done.

Dad appeared at the back door as Jake was eating his toast. He came in and started washing his hands at the sink. 'I thought you might want to go and say goodbye to Jessie and Ted before we go,' he said. 'There's time if we hurry.'

Jake thought about it for a moment. The whole thing felt like a bad dream, especially now that he was rushing to pack and get away on time, just as he had to do at the end of every holiday. He would return to Auckland, and nobody there would ever believe what had happened to him. Part of him wanted to leave without looking back, to just forget the events of yesterday and the trouble he had caused. But none of it was Jessie or Ted's fault.

'Sure,' he said.

'Great,' said Dad. 'I'll finish up here. The car's unlocked. Go and put your bag in and I'll be down in a minute.'

Jake looked at his father's back as he cleaned up and wondered if they would talk about what had happened. At the moment, his father seemed to be concentrating hard on trying to forget, to erase all traces of Cara, so Jake was surprised Dad wanted to go anywhere near Red Rocks.

'Are you sure you don't mind?' he asked. 'Aren't you worried you might see Cara?'

Dad turned around, drying his hands on a tea towel. 'You're pretty smart, you know that? Actually, I was thinking of waiting in the car.' He reached out a hand as if to ruffle Jake's hair, then appeared to change his mind. 'I swear you've grown since you've been here,' he said. 'You'll be taller than me in no time. I'd better watch out!'

Outside, Jake opened the boot of Dad's car and heaved his bag into it. As he slammed it shut, he felt something nudging the back of his legs.

'Heel, Sam!' came a voice, and Jake turned around to see a grey-haired man with a cloth cap on his head, and at the end of the lead in his hand, snuffling around Jake's feet, the Golden Lab from down the road.

Jake crouched down and rubbed the dog's ears. 'Hey, boy,' he said.

The man smiled and waited while Jake patted his dog. 'He obviously likes you.'

Jake stared into the dog's trusting brown eyes and felt a stab of guilt. He stood up and looked the owner in the face, resisting the urge to hang his head.

'I saw some boys teasing him a while ago,' he said. 'I'm sorry, I should have told you.'

'Ah, those little thugs,' said the man. 'They just about choked the neighbour's dog yesterday. Don't worry, they got caught. The police even got involved. Those kids won't be hurting any animals again in a hurry. And don't worry, Sam here's still as happy as a clam. No real harm done.'

Sam's tongue was hanging out and he was looking at Jake expectantly. What was going on behind those soft eyes? Suddenly, Jake got the certain feeling the dog had forgiven him, that they understood each other. After all, they'd both been on the receiving end of the bullying and survived. And Jake had stood up to the boys eventually. Maybe he'd even be able to stand up to the bullies at school next term. He certainly felt ready for them. He gave the dog a last pat and it trotted off with its owner towards the beach.

It was hard to believe it was nearly two weeks ago that he'd first encountered Mark and Dan. And yet, how was it *only* two weeks ago? So much had happened, he felt as though he'd been here for months. And Jessie had grown so much — it was as if years had passed. He felt older himself. Not a little kid any more.

'Right, we're off.' The front door banged behind Dad. He had put on a clean shirt and was a different man from the one who had hunched on the couch last night. Only the wound on his cheek was left as an outward reminder.

Jake turned and looked back at the little cottage, at his father's writing shed, with its boarded-up window, peeking over the top. He never knew where Dad would be living each time he came; he moved around a lot. He hoped it would be this place, but for all he knew it could be miles away.

'I've been meaning to tell you,' said Dad, as though reading his mind. 'I've been offered a new place, cheaper rent. I wasn't going to take it, but now I think the change will do me good. It's in Paremata. You'll love it. I've got a boat shed to write in. If the dinghy can be fixed, we can take it and go fishing there, too.' He gave a wry smile. 'No seals there, though.'

Jake just nodded and got into the car. He had learned not to get too attached to his father's houses. He hoped Dad wouldn't be too lonely without him, but he didn't know how to say it out loud.

The car rolled into the car park near Ted's, and Jake got out. His whole body was sore and scraped from his adventures, and he was looking forward to having a rest to let his wounds heal. The cliffs looked huge today, and the wind was up again, churning the grey sky. This is how he would always remember the road out to Red Rocks — windswept and sullen.

He started walking away, but Dad's door opened suddenly.

'Wait!' he called. 'I'll come with you. Not sure I can trust you to be back on time.' As his father laid a hand on his shoulder, Jake wondered if, after everything that had happened, Dad still wanted to protect him and was just making an excuse to accompany him. Or maybe he really did want to risk seeing Cara and was using Jake to give him strength, make him brave. Either way, Jake was glad to have the company.

To catch the plane in time, they needed to set off at a brisk pace. Jake's legs ached as he walked, and he longed to slow down. Dad took big strides, despite the fact he must have been feeling just as stiff as Jake was after the events of the previous day. Together, they ignored their pain and marched onwards.

Jake's eyes searched the clumps of kelp and the foamy sea for a sign of the seals, but there were none that he could see. He couldn't help noticing that Dad did the same.

They passed the wreckage of Jake's bike as they walked along the road.

'Don't worry,' said his dad, 'I'll have it fixed up good as new for the next time you come down.'

Smoke rolled from the chimney of Ted's hut and up towards the cliffs. Ted took a long time to open the door, and when he did he looked as though he had been asleep. His eyes were bleary and he had new creases on his face. Jake remembered how easy it had been to doze off on that little bed by the wood stove. Ted looked at them blankly for a moment, then his face brightened and he cracked a wide smile, showing his broken yellowed teeth.

'Am I glad to see you!'

Dad took a surprised step backwards as Ted rushed forward with his fingers outstretched. The two men shook hands, Ted clasping Dad's with both of his own. Jake saw understanding dawn on his father's face: that here was a man who had loved a selkie and lost her, along with his children. Dad hadn't believed the story when Jake had told him, but Jake realised that deep down his father now knew it to be true. Dad's whole body relaxed, and for a moment the haunted look bubbled to the surface again while Ted pumped his hand up and down.

'Thank you,' said Dad. 'Just . . . thank you.'

Jake smiled to himself. It was as if the two men had told each other their life stories without ever exchanging a word.

'Is Jessie here?' he asked.

'Come in, come in,' said Ted, letting go of Dad's hand and shuffling back with a sigh.

The room looked much the same as the last time Jake saw it. Shabby, with frayed and mended furniture, and every surface covered, but Jake could see now that the place was tidy and well cared for in its own way. It always smelt fresh and clean despite the age and condition of the house. The ever-present rack of clothes was drying by the fire. Jake could see the shorts and jersey Jessie had been wearing, and also the old overcoat Cara had worn. Dad seemed about to speak, but closed his mouth when he spotted the coat. He stared at it for a few seconds before tearing his gaze away.

Ted gestured around the room. 'As you can see,' he said, 'Jessie's not here.'

Jake flicked a glance at his father, then said, 'Will you go and get her?'

'No, young fella,' said Ted. 'I can't do that, not today. She's gone home as well. She might be back next year, she might not.'

'Oh, what a pity,' said Dad. 'I'm sorry we missed her.' He laid a hand on Jake's shoulder. 'Maybe Jake can come and visit her next year. We're moving away, but it might be possible.'

It was at that moment that Jake realised his father had no idea what Jessie was. If he knew, Jake didn't think he would let him be friends with her any more, not after what had happened with Cara.

'I don't know,' said Ted. 'I reckon she might have changed by then. You know how kids are. They grow up so fast.' Ted winked at Jake, who felt himself blushing.

'Well, all right, Ted,' said Dad. 'We'll leave you to it. I might see you sometime if this idea gets off the ground for my book, the one about the south coast. I'll have to talk to my publishers about it, of course. They're pretty fickle.' He sighed. 'Although I'm having second thoughts about it myself. Maybe it's best not to examine things too closely, eh?'

'That's true,' said Ted, smiling his raggedy smile.

Jake forced a smile back and took a last look around the cosy cottage. Would he ever see it, or Ted, again? He wished he'd had a chance to see Jessie one last time. Even if she returned next year, she would be grown up, while he would still be stuck as a kid. That was just too crazy to think about.

On the way back to the car, Dad hoisted the bike onto his shoulders. The waves washed the stones, and Jake thought back to that first day, when it sounded as if the water and the rocks were carrying on a conversation, telling each other stories of what they'd seen.

'You okay?' asked Dad.

'Yeah,' said Jake. 'I wanted to say goodbye to her, but that's okay.'

As he said it, he heard a splashing sound coming from the water.

'Well, someone's come to say goodbye to you, anyway,' said Dad, looking alarmed at first, then relaxing. 'I wonder if it's the one we saw when we were out fishing?'

Jake looked: a seal danced in the water beside them.

'I think it is.' As he spoke, the seal launched itself in the air, spiralled around and disappeared. When it emerged again, moments later, it rolled onto its side and raised a flipper, as if in a wave. Jake waved back and smiled.

Acknowledgements

I am grateful to Creative New Zealand for a 'quick response' grant, which enabled me to write with two small children. Thanks to the following people for helpful feedback at various stages: Tania Roxborogh, Pippi Priestley-King & Rebecca Priestley, James Gracewood-Easther and Ros Henry (otherwise known as Mum); my wonderful (and tireless) agents, Vivien Green and Gaia Banks; the fabulous team at Random House New Zealand, in particular Jenny Hellen, for her boundless support, patience and enthusiasm; editor Jolisa Gracewood, especially for taking queries at midnight before the final manuscript was due; Peter Rutherford for moral support and incredibly insightful creative input, and my children, Tom and AJ Rutherford, who have always been the readers I had in mind while writing this book, despite only being aged five and two when I finished it. Finally I'd like to thank a place: the windy, wonderful south coast of Wellington, where I have done some of my best and most important thinking, and where I walked as a new mother with a baby and was bowled over by the unexpected idea for the story of *Red Rocks*.

About the author

Rachael King is the author of two novels for adults: *Magpie Hall* and *The Sound of Butterflies*, which won the award for the best first novel at the 2007 Montana Book Awards and was published in ten languages. The idea for *Red Rocks* came to her as she walked her first baby son around Wellington's wild south coast and thought it a place where magic could happen. Now with two sons, she wanted to write down the story for them and is thrilled to share it with other children as well. In 2008 Rachael was the Ursula Bethell Writer in Residence at Canterbury University, and she has lived in Christchurch ever since.